15.

Includes Center for Media and Public Affairs' Newest Report
on Media Coverage of the Catholic Church

Anti-Catholicism
in
American Culture

Edited by
Robert P. Lockwood

Our Sunday Visitor Publishing Division
Our Sunday Visitor, Inc.
Huntington, Indiana 46750

International Standard Book Number: 0-87973-342-X
Library of Congress Catalog Card Number: 99-75027

Cover design by Monica Haneline;
based on a *Harper's Weekly* editorial cartoon by Thomas Nast
PRINTED IN THE UNITED STATES OF AMERICA

Table of Contents

Introduction

Anti-Catholicism arrived in America with the Pilgrims in 1620. While it is a prejudice that has existed in every decade of the American experience, anti-Catholicism is in many ways stronger now than it has ever been. It is a powerful force in art, business, academics, entertainment, politics, commentary, and news reporting. It is not only America's most persistent prejudice but also its most accepted. It remains the last refuge of legitimate bigotry, understood as not only correct in its assumptions but also normative to enlightened thought.

Strong words, and not without dissent. Most non-Catholics — and many Catholics — can vaguely recall their history books telling them that at one time in Boston there were signs outside factories stating that "No Irish Need Apply." They might recall hearing or reading that Al Smith lost to Herbert Hoover in the 1928 presidential campaign because he was Catholic. They might even know that there was a political party prior to the Civil War called the "Know Nothings" who did not like Catholics. (They were called "Know Nothings" because when asked about their beliefs or activities, they would allegedly respond that they "know nothing," a myth some historians dismiss.) But that is about the extent of the common knowledge of anti-Catholicism in American culture, and most would see it as a historical relic that effectively ended when John F. Kennedy was elected president in 1960.

On April 7, 1998, ABC aired during Holy Week a sitcom called *That's Life*. The following description is from the Catholic League's *1998 Report on Anti-Catholicism:*

> The show began with the usual denigration of Church teaching — criticisms of "the way the Catholic

Church treats women, and their views on abortion, homosexuality, censorship." The obligatory allusion to priests as child molesters was of course thrown in: "Father Doyle said he needs another altar boy." "Yeah, well, he does go through them." Defenders of the Church were predictably inept: "It don't matter if you know what you are saying — as long as you believe it." We heard how there is "no real spiritual salvation going on" in the Church, and how "the Church is dying because everybody our age with a reasonable amount of intelligence has left."

A 10-year-old boy, taken to church by his godfather, described why he liked the experience. Referring to the stained glass windows, he said: "They show Jesus carrying the cross, totally bruised up, and the soldiers are hitting him. . . . Imagine the blood comes spurting out of it like a hose. I mean, whack, whack, whack, sss. . . ."

Taking a piece of bread at the dinner table, the boy asked, "Wouldn't it be cool if this bread actually transformed into the body of Christ? You know, like you were actually eating a body? And after he eats it he says, 'Drink this, for this is my blood.' " Later, the boy asked his godfather, "Can we go over the Stations of the Cross? I want to know when the soldier stabs Jesus in the ribs." Then he observed, "Did you know the Vatican has see-through coffins of saints so you can see their decaying bones?" Finally, the confessional is referred to as "like a spiritual toilet."

When the Catholic League protested, ABC responded with a one-sentence letter, stating that the show was not intended "to offend any religious denomination."

Other than the sheer tastelessness of such a show, what is interesting about the ABC production is how closely it mirrored centuries of anti-Catholic prejudice. As outlined in the first chapter on the evolution of anti-Catholicism, the script writers of *That's Life* were echoing prejudices that would have been understood in colonial America: The Catholic Church is based on bizarre, medieval beliefs; it is sexually unnatural in its practices, yet at the same time libertine in its clergy and religious; the laity are kept in ignorance by a repressive hierarchy and are saved only when exposed to reasonable thought; Catholic ritual is essentially macabre, mere superstitious ritual masquerading as religion. Finally, as noted in ABC's dismissive response, such a prejudicial representation of Catholicism can hardly be deemed "to offend any religious denomination." Anti-Catholicism and caricatures of Catholicism are a part of the American cultural landscape that no right-thinking person could possibly identify with something as ugly as bigotry.

While a short-lived sitcom may seem an unlikely beginning to a study of anti-Catholicism, it reminds us that this bigotry is neither exceptional nor a vanished part of the American past. It is not merely the product of old ignorance or misguided ethnic antipathy. Rather, it is central to the way Americans think and fundamental to American culture. Anti-Catholic assumptions are part of the American mind-set with a shared vocabulary and a shared reasoning process. The alleged humor in *That's Life* worked because anyone in the audience would understand it. They would comprehend the joke because the presumptions about Catholics and Catholic beliefs are part of their intellectual and emotional makeup. Anti-Catholicism is normative to American thinking, a part of our American heritage.

In 1993, Our Sunday Visitor released *Anti-Catholicism in the Media: An Examination of Whether Elite News Organizations Are Biased Against the Church*. That book was based on a study commissioned by the Catholic League for Religious and Civil Rights and the Knights of Columbus. The study, conducted by the Center for Media and Public Affairs, was an examination of leading American news organizations to determine whether or not they exhibited bias in reporting on the Catholic Church. *Anti-Catholicism in the Media* included commentaries and papers given at a seminar based on the study held at the National Press Club in Washington, D.C., in September, 1991.

That first study by the Center for Media and Public Affairs examined coverage of the Catholic Church in three five-year periods from 1964 through 1988 by *The New York Times, The Washington Post, Time* magazine, and *CBS Evening News.* Among the major conclusions of the first study were that in most controversies involving Catholic teachings, the Church came out on the losing side of the issue in an allegedly objective press. Controversies within the Church were always presented as conflicts between a hidebound institutional hierarchy against brave, tireless, and democratic reformers. The Church was consistently characterized as conservative in theology with "authoritarian forms of control, and an anachronistic approach to contemporary society." The debate over the moral teachings of the Church in matters of sexuality was most often portrayed as the hierarchy engaged in a losing battle to impose its benighted views on the laity, who were in profound disagreement. News stories consistently favored decentralization of Church authority, while Church involvement in political debates was always viewed as a threat to separation of Church and State. In summary, the Church was most often portrayed as an oppressive and authoritarian institution, and at the same time irrelevant to contemporary society.

The Catholic League for Religious and Civil Rights and Our Sunday Visitor asked the Center for Media and Public Affairs to conduct a new study of leading print and broadcast outlets in the 1990s. The second study was intended to update

the 1991 report, expand its coverage to additional media outlets, and investigate how anti-Catholicism in the media might
have changed in recent years. ABC and NBC evening news
broadcasts were added to the study, while newspapers were
expanded to include *USA Today*. *U.S. News & World Report*
and *Newsweek* were added to *Time* magazine among the
newsweeklies. The study was conducted on news items that
appeared from 1994 through 1998.

The results of this new study are contained in Part II of
this book. Essentially, the new study found that the role of
women in the Church had become virtually the dominant issue. The first study found a host of issues — authority, the role
of the laity, sexual morality, issues of Church and State, birth
control, minorities, treatment of internal disputes, alleged issues of freedom of expression, ecumenical relations, dissent
— as grist for the journalistic mill, with a firm bias against
traditional Catholic positions. The new study found that, for
the most part, such issues evinced little interest. Coverage focused almost solely on a media portrayal of a Catholic Church
that oppresses women in some ill-defined fashion. Three out
of four stories criticized the Church's treatment of women.
According to the study, "fully 90 percent of sources on TV
news were critical of the Church" in this area.

As with the 1993 report, there will certainly be disagreement in interpreting the results of this new study. Some will
point to declining coverage of the Church as evidence that the
"Religious Right" takes greater heat now from the media. It
can also be argued, as Russell Shaw postulates in his contribution to this book, that anti-Catholicism has taken a new form
in the media. It is not so much open hostility as evidenced in
the past, but a matter of allying with internal Catholic dissent
against the magisterium of the Church.

Shaw has an intriguing analysis. In effect, it points to a

"Stockholm syndrome" among Catholics in American culture. So pervasive is anti-Catholic thought and assumptions within American culture that they have become absorbed within Catholics themselves. Many Catholics have simply succumbed to the anti-Catholic environment and become hostages to it. They are "cultural soupers," like the Irish who allegedly left the Church in the Great Famine in exchange for a bowl of soup. But instead of Protestant missionaries engaging in a charade of altruism, it is journalists trading external objectivity for internal manipulation of Catholic dissent, with the cooperation of the dissenters.

In Part I of *Anti-Catholicism in American Culture*, the history and contemporary state of anti-Catholicism, with emphasis on representation in the media, is examined. A practical essay by Bill Donohue of the Catholic League on how best to respond to anti-Catholicism concludes this section. There is no one in the country that could give better advice. In Part II, the full text of the study by the Center for Media and Public Affairs, *Media Coverage of the Catholic Church 1963-1968,* is presented. Also included is the executive summary from the first study. However, for a full understanding of the issue, a review of the complete text of the first study and the papers from the 1991 seminar in *Anti-Catholicism in the Media* is strongly recommended.

* * *

Let me acknowledge a number of people involved in the creation of this book. First, Russ Shaw must be thanked for suggesting the idea of revisiting the study on anti-Catholicism in the media. Happily, it was a suggestion shared not only with me but also with Bob Lichter of the Center for Media and Public Affairs, who responded enthusiastically. Bill Donohue was supportive from the start, offering helpful suggestions as well as full cooperation and sponsorship by the Catholic League.

Veteran reporter Lou Baldwin accepted his assignment with enthusiasm over a lovely dinner in Philadelphia. Rick Hinshaw made his contribution even as he was on his way to what will surely be remarkable service for the New York State Catholic Conference. Mike Dubruiel of Our Sunday Visitor made certain that the manuscript was put together in a timely fashion.

This study and book would not have been possible without the support of the Board of Directors of Our Sunday Visitor, Inc., who graciously supplied the necessary resources. Finally, a prayer in memory of the founder of Our Sunday Visitor, Archbishop John F. Noll (1875-1956). He would have relished the discussion.

ROBERT P. LOCKWOOD

PART

✦

I

CHAPTER ✧ 1

The Evolution of Anti-Catholicism in the United States

By Robert P. Lockwood

I

It was an ill-fated conspiracy with disastrous consequences. On November 5, 1605, a small group of fanatic Catholics planned to blow up the House of Parliament in London, killing the assembled leadership and assassinating King James I. Suffering under the anti-Catholic disabilities begun by the Tudor King Henry VIII and formalized under his daughter Elizabeth, English Catholics had hoped for relief from the new Stuart king and his allegedly Catholic wife. When it became clear that a wider toleration was not to be, the plot was hatched among a few desperate men.

From a rented building, the conspirators dug a trench to a cellar beneath the House of Parliament. That room was filled with barrels of gunpowder. One of the conspirators, Guy Fawkes, was to set off the charge. The dissidents hoped that the ensuing destruction would lead to a Catholic uprising in England and an invasion from Europe. The conspiracy was discovered, Fawkes was arrested in the cellar, and, under torture, revealed the names of his fellow conspirators. Those who were not killed resisting arrest were eventually executed, including a few who had little or nothing to do with what became popularly known as the "Gunpowder Plot."

The anti-Catholic atmosphere in England since Henry VIII's break with Rome had been primarily a top-down affair up until the Gunpowder Plot. Even the possibility of invasion by the Spanish Armada in 1588 had served to unify English

15

Catholics against the Spanish threat, rather than engender an uprising on their part or increased persecution from a government desperate for any internal ally. The anti-Catholic laws in place prior to the Gunpowder Plot were cruel, but they were aimed primarily at priests, who were to be tortured and killed if found in England. The laity who remained quietly faithful to Rome were generally left in peace and the restrictions placed upon them lackadaisically enforced. Many Catholics publicly attended Anglican services while maintaining the "olde faith" in private. Even the publicly identified "recusant" Catholics — those who actually refused to attend Protestant services and were formally fined — were able to quietly go about their business.

This popular quietude over the Catholic issue was of great concern to the English government as Queen Elizabeth's rule neared an end in 1603. Assuming that Catholics were a hidden army that would support invasion from the Catholic royal houses of Europe, they were viewed as a potentially treasonous alien presence. The Gunpowder Plot gave the government the perfect opportunity to enhance legal restrictions on Catholics and at the same time encourage on a popular level an anti-Catholicism that would dominate popular English culture to our day.

In the wake of the Gunpowder Plot, "Catholics could no longer practice law, nor serve in the Army or Navy as officers. No recusant could act as either executor of a will, guardian to a minor, nor even possess a weapon except in cases of self-defense. Catholics could not receive a university degree, could not vote in local elections or in parliamentary elections. All this on top of the spiritual penalties by which Catholics were ordered to marry in the Anglican church, take their children there for baptism, and finally rest in its burial grounds. . . . (A) profound prejudice against Papists . . . remained lurking in the popular conscience after 1605, ready to emerge from its depths at any hint of leniency towards them. For many Protestants, a declaration of February, 1606, on the subject of the Plot by Sir Thomas Smith summed the matter up: 'this bloody stain and mark will never be washed out of the Popish religion.' It was a stain that would be passed on to unborn generations. It was the alleged 'foreign' nature of Catholicism — ruled by an alien Pope based in Rome — which made it perennially vulnerable to attack. . . . In 1651 Milton called Catholicism not so much a religion as 'a (foreign) priestly despotism under the cloak of religion arrayed in the spoils of temporal power.' He was on firm ground that would not be surrendered by every Protestant until the late twentieth century (if then)" (*Faith and Treason: The Story of the Gunpowder Plot*, Antonia Fraser, Doubleday, 1996).

Perhaps the most well-known memorial to the Gunpowder Plot was the popular celebration of Guy Fawkes Day each November 5 with bonfires used to burn the pope in effigy. According to Fraser, anti-Catholic celebrations on each November the fifth became a virtual high holy day in England. Over the centuries, "celebrations waxed and waned according to the waves of anti-Catholicism which periodically shook England. Any apparent support given to that dangerous foreign-based religion, and renewed threat from its supporters, was enough to make the annual bonfires burn brighter."

Guy Fawkes Day was celebrated in the New World colonies up until the American Revolution. It was particularly popular in New England, and Fraser reports that it was "a special feature of Boston life among the 'lower elements.' " Generally referred to as "Pope Day," its only reference in American history is during the Revolution. General George Washington issued an order in 1775 banning his troops from burning the pope in effigy on November 5 as a "ridiculous and childish custom," particularly at a time when Catholic French Canadians were being wooed as allies against England. It lingered on after the Revolution in certain areas, but Guy Fawkes Day eventually disappeared in America.

For King James I, "more fateful in the long run than the amateurish Gunpowder plot," Father Marvin O'Connell wrote, "was the conference at Hampton Court twenty months before, at which the Puritan minority — dormant during Elizabeth's last years but far from dead — presented a list of grievances against the Established Church" (*The Counter Reformation,* Harper and Row, 1974). It would be this Puritan minority that would have the head of James's son, King Charles I, on January 30, 1649.

It was only fifteen years after the unmasking of The Gunpowder Plot — twenty-nine years before Charles lost his head — that the Puritans came to America in 1620 to establish the Plymouth Colony. And they brought with them a hatred of Catholicism that was strongly affected by the populist anti-Catholicism engendered in the wake of the Gunpowder Plot. This anti-Catholicism would become an integral part of American culture and thought, affecting both as much today as when the Pilgrims first saw Cape Cod.

II

January 1, 1998, Darlington, S.C. — The News and Press ran an editorial which used a legitimate issue — a lenient sentence given to a priest convicted of sexually molesting a boy — as an excuse for a vicious and wide-ranging anti-Catholic diatribe. The editorial claimed that "this incident is but the latest over hundreds of years involving priests and nuns sworn to celibacy. There are unknown nameless infants buried in convents all over the world." . . . In response to a torrent of criticism, the editor reran the editorial on January 22 . . . declaring, "We do not apologize for it." — 1998 Report on

Anti-Catholicism, *Catholic League for Religious and Civil Rights*

Anti-Catholicism is fundamental to the culture of the United States. It found its birth in the anti-Catholic propaganda of the English government in the late 1500s and early 1600s when the Church was painted as the enemy of enlightened thought and an alien presence eager to overthrow the rights of Englishmen. It was this popular anti-Catholicism that would be transported to the English colonies in the New World. As those colonies severed their formal ties with England in the American Revolution, they did not abandon an essentially English pattern of thought and culture that carried this baggage of anti-Catholicism. As virtually every colony had some form of Catholic disabilities in their fundamental charters — denying Catholics the right to hold office or freedom to practice their faith — many of the new states in the union would have similar legislation on the books, if not formally enforced. (Only four of the original thirteen states removed penal laws against Catholics. New Hampshire would not formally remove its law barring Catholics from public office until late in the nineteenth century.)

Like any other prejudice, anti-Catholicism is a fundamental judgment that defines a group of people as a whole by negative and preconceived assumptions as to their thought, motives, and actions. The bigot creates these assumptions — or inherits them — and they are used as the basis of all judgments on a particular group. These assumptions allow the bigot to dismiss out-of-hand any actions or positions of the group by assigning predetermined motives, and to see that group as inherently inferior, foreign to the majority, and less worthy — or less trustworthy — of the rights and privileges of the majority. In the specific case of anti-Catholicism, this prejudice is also viewed as correct, normative, and universally shared. It is acceptable, useful in public debate, and understood to be the product of an enlightened mind.

Anti-Catholicism is not disagreement with what the Church believes and teaches, even when forcefully — or satirically — expressed. It is not heated theological disputes and expressions of negative judgments on Church activities or public positions. Anti-Catholicism, particularly as seen in the media, is the blind use of negative generalizations, invented history, vicious stereotypes, appeals to shared prejudices, applications of underlying base motives without proof, misrepresentations of religious beliefs, or purposeful and vicious denigration of religious beliefs, all with the intent of ridiculing, dismissing, or publicly attacking Catholic positions or applications of belief in the public square without actively engaging the actual issues or positions involved.

The elements that make up popular anti-Catholicism in the American culture are not much different today than when Guy Fawkes was hanged from the scaffold for his part in the plot on the king's life. The primary elements of anti-Catholicism are shared assumptions that can be found throughout the history of the Church in the United States. They are stereotypes relished in colonial times, and assumed in contemporary news and entertainment media.

CATHOLICS AS ANTI-ENLIGHTENMENT • Catholics and Catholicism are portrayed as essentially anti-intellectual, with the faith a collection of meaningless superstitions and thoughtless rituals that are a product of a pre-enlightened era. While the driving force behind this stereotype today is secular thought, its roots are essentially in the Protestant Reformation ridicule of the "crosses and idle ceremonies of popery." As a prominent Boston minister referred to John Carroll, the first bishop of the United States: "It seems strange that a man of sense should be so zealous in the cause of nonsense." Similarly, a contemporary New York publisher would publicly dismiss in *The New York Times* Pope John Paul II's *Crossing the Threshold of Hope* as representing a sixteenth-century Weltanshauung, or world view, that is irrelevant to the modern mind. Most common today, this view portrays Catholicism as an inherent enemy of any new trend in society and contemporary thought, and thus its views on such matters to be readily dismissed. It is also the source of routine acceptance of mockery and ridicule of Catholic religious ritual, practices, and beliefs, since they are viewed as merely superstitious relics from a bygone era.

CATHOLICISM AS ANTI-DEMOCRATIC • Throughout American history, the Catholic Church and Catholics were portrayed as forces of evil, intent on destroying individual freedom. In the 1700s, 1800s, and early 1900s, this form of anti-Catholicism portrayed Catholics as dominated by the pope and his Jesuit minions. Today it portrays lay Catholics as incapable of independent thought and, as they slavishly subscribe to arcane religious belief, unworthy and unable to function in a free society. By the very nature of the Church, Catholics are inherently sworn enemies of free institutions. In the past, this was the belief behind various "test acts" for public office that required Catholics to swear an oath that they would not have an allegiance to any "foreign power" (the pope), as this would compromise their ability to judge according to democratic norms. It is common today where Catholics are generally still asked to deny the influence of their Catholicity in holding public office, serving as justices, lawyers, or in the medical profession, or particularly in journalism. (During the public impeachment debate over President Clinton's activities, presidential supporters in the press argued that certain news commentators had compromised their objectivity because of their Catholicity, which made them overly scrupulous in matters of sexual morality.) This prejudice assumes Catholics cannot abide by the rules of a democratic society and will attempt to usurp these rules by forcing a theocratic model on America whenever possible. It allows for out-of-hand rejection of Catholic positions in the public square as being inherently un-American in their motives, if not in the positions themselves.

POWER IS THE SOLE DRIVING FORCE OF CATHOLICISM • In the heady days just prior to the American Revolution, anti-Catholicism was a card often played to stir up resistance to the monarchy. Passage of the Quebec Act by Parliament — which guaranteed freedom of religion to French Catholic Canadians in Quebec, considered the seat of the Antichrist by New Englanders — provoked this response: "We may live to see our churches converted to masshouses and our lands plundered for tythes for the support of a Popish clergy. The Inquisition may erect her standard in Pennsylvania, and the city of Philadelphia may yet experience the carnage of St. Bartholomew's Day." A constant in anti-Catholic propaganda was that the Catholic Church represented tyranny, and all its actions were based on a grab for secular power. Common to the anti-Catholic literature of the 1800s and 1900s was the claim that the Catholic hierarchy was out to take over or to destroy the public school system, which was seen as the bastion of Protestant American culture. Paul Blanshard made the best-seller list in the 1950s with his ominous warnings of a "Catholic power" in America. Today, particularly in the press, Catholic teaching is rarely reported on its face value. Religious or faith-based motives are dismissed and alternatives for Catholic action are presented as the desire to oppress or as a means to grab for secular power. In a July 3, 1998, edition of *The Day,* a daily paper in New London, Connecticut, a commentary on a papal encyclical compared papal teaching to oppressive Communist regimes. In June, 1998, a religion writer for the *Palm Beach Post* called the Catholic Church "the world's oldest totalitarian state."

CATHOLICISM IS THE RELIGION OF INFERIOR RACES • The signs with the words "No Irish Need Apply" were common in Boston throughout the 1700s, 1800s, and 1900s. Catholicism was identified as the religion of people deemed inferior by the white Anglo-Saxon Protestant establishment. The wave of poor Irish Catholic immigrants that began in the 1830s, and became a virtual deluge after the Irish famine years of the 1840s, bolstered a nativist political movement that would have a strong undercurrent throughout American social history. Catholic Italian and Eastern European immigration in the late 1800s and early 1900s would lead to anti-immigration laws designed to keep America the great white Protestant experiment. Margaret Sanger's birth control movement began as a reaction against the "breeding habits" of these poor Catholic immigrants of inferior race who would "take over" white America. While such movements and legislation were also aimed at curtailing non-Catholic Asians and European Jews, the primary fears centered on races deemed inferior and infected with a foreign religion. Today, anti-immigration arguments are generally aimed at the predominantly Catholic immigrants from Mexico and the rest of Latin America. In an April 4, 1998, issue of the *Pittsburgh Tribune-Review*, writer Donald Collins ripped the Church, among other things, for its immigration positions and "deplored the fact that 90 percent of all new immigrants to the United States are Catholic" (*1998 Report on Anti-Catholicism*).

A FAITH ALIEN TO AMERICA • "Yet even the most liberal republicans and most indifferent dissenters had little use for Roman Catholics. English-speaking peoples regarded Catholics as superstitious, slavishly subservient to the pope and his Jesuit minions, and treacherous allies of the country's enemies during her hours of supreme crisis" (*Public Catholicism*, David

O'Brien, Macmillan, 1989). Similar to the fear of inferior races, Catholicism was viewed as an alien or foreign presence within the colonies and within the United States. Catholics represented something foreign to the American experience and have always been considered vaguely threatening strangers in our midst. In the early seventeenth-century British propaganda machine, it was argued that the Catholics in Britain would be a ready source for alliance with the Spanish or French monarchies. (It was proposed in 1613 that Catholics in England be forced to wear a red stocking cap that would allow them to be readily identified in public and their activities monitored.) In the United States, this took on less of a political fear and more of a social concern. There were some sentiments expressed about Catholic loyalty in the Spanish-American War. There were also fears that Catholics would support the German Triple Alliance in World War I because of Pope Benedict XV's Italian heritage and the papacy's historic ties to the Hapsburg emperors of Austro-Hungary, as well as the Anglophobia of the Irish Catholic Americans. For the most part, however, this foreign and alien concept of Catholics expressed itself more in religious terms, with Catholicism as a faith contrary to true Americanism. The Catholic faith was seen as essentially alien to the predominant Protestant culture. Benedict Arnold described a Mass attended by leaders of Congress and wondered: "Do you know that the eye which guides this pen lately saw your mean and profligate Congress at Mass for the soul of a Roman Catholic in Purgatory, and participating in the rites of a Church against whose anti-Christ corruption your pious ancestors would bear witness with their blood?" The revised Ku Klux Klan of the early twentieth century protested vehemently against the alien Catholic religion growing on American soil. Allegations of the alleged dual citizenship of Catholics were widespread in the 1950s and raised prominently in the 1960 presidential elections. In contemporary media coverage this is often seen in the need to identify Catholics by their faith when no other person within a story is identified by religious preference or denomination. It is seen in the underlying assumption that Catholics as individual Americans are legitimately considered second-class citizens because of their "alien" religion. If they take positions contrary to the prevailing sentiment, such second-class status can be expected once again. This is an argument consistently used on the editorial pages of *The New York Times* when the Church speaks out on issues such as abortion or euthanasia. In effect, the argument is that if the Church refuses to keep its benighted views to itself, it can only expect a bigoted response and deservedly so. It is a curious argument in that it blames bigotry on the victim.

SEXUAL PROFLIGACY, PRUDERY • The most curious anti-Catholic stereotype arises in regard to sexual practices. The relationship of Catholicism and sexuality has been a bedrock of anti-Catholic assumptions since Henry VIII. On the one hand, because of the practice of priestly celibacy, Catholicism is viewed as an unhealthy, sexually repressed faith with unmanly leadership and prudish laity. At the same time, Catholics are viewed from the Margaret Sanger perspective as unthinking breeders, while its clergy are perceived as lascivious predators of the young and innocent. Again, this is a prejudice that transcends time. English hate literature is filled with rutting Irish, copulating priests and nuns, and, at the same time, innocent rubes grown old and out-of-touch because of their unnatural celibate lifestyle. In America, anti-Catholic literature was so strewn with sexual deviancy that it was often referred to as "Puritan Pornography." *The Awful Disclosures of Maria Monk*, alleging horrible sexual deviancies in a convent in Montreal, was first published in 1835 and became a best-seller second only to the Bible in American religious publishing. Though proven to be totally false, the book became a reason for ongoing raids on convents to "free" young women from sexual slavery. Today, this dual anti-Catholic assumption thrives. The pope, the hierarchy, and the clergy are portrayed as old celibate males out of touch with reality. At the same time, it is argued that they are crass sexual predators. This has been seen in the coverage of the issue of priestly pedophilia, where such aberrations are portrayed not only as "common" among Catholic clergy but also as a natural result of an unnatural celibacy. While one case of priestly pedophilia is one case too many, this story took on a life of its own that far outweighed the depth of the problem. While it has been shown that priests are less likely to engage in pedophilia than the general population, the cases extant have allowed the media to engage in a surfeit of anti-Catholicism. Yet with all these alleged sexual scandals, the Church is most often portrayed as a behind-the-times collection of prudes who are unnaturally sexually repressed.

THE DELUDED CATHOLIC • In a similar self-contradictory expression of anti-Catholicism, Catholics have long been portrayed as ignorant dupes marching in lockstep at the behest of their hierarchical masters. Yet, at the same time, most Catholics are portrayed as not believing what the Church teaches, if those teachings stand in contrast to the conventional cultural wisdom. In old English anti-Catholic propaganda, this involved the fear that Catholics were always at the beck and call of the pope, who would order them to rise up in revolution, destroy their Protestant monarchy, and restore the true faith to England. Similarly, in United States history there were numerous instances of claims of a Catholic uprising about to happen. The American Patriotic Association (APA) became enormously powerful in the Midwest in the 1890s with its claim of an imminent armed Catholic uprising on the command of Jesuits and the hierarchy. Yet, at the same time, Catholics were universally proclaimed to be ignorant of any real tenets of their faith and Christianity. If one could only expose them to the actual Church teaching, they would see its inherent errors and be saved from Catholic perdition. Today, that same type of dualism is common to coverage of the Catholic Church. When members of the hierarchy issue statements on contemporary social issues such as abortion or euthanasia, commentators are quick to register the complaint that the hierarchy are telling Catholics how to vote and are violating the separation of Church and State. "After Cardinal Anthony Bevilacqua voiced his opposition to Philadelphia's same-sex 'life partnership' legislation, the *Northeast Times* . . . accused him of crossing the line between Church and State, and scolded him for entering 'the public pulpit' instead of restricting himself to 'those on the altar of churches' " (*1998 Report on Anti-Catholicism*). At the same time, any coverage of a papal visit to a country is quick to allege that while the pope is personally popular among Catholics, none believe in his message, particularly if it involves traditional Catholic positions on abortion or sexual morality.

III

Those seven general anti-Catholic assumptions are common to the American experience and make up the general assumptions that the media utilize when dealing with the Catholic Church and Catholics today. These assumptions have been remarkably stable throughout the history of the Church in the United States and can be found in virtually any era. They have been employed both together and individually as they apply to specific issues of each era. They have operated, however, in a continuum and are indelibly stamped on our collective American conscience.

In colonial days, anti-Catholicism was a direct outgrowth of the English experience, following the customs and laws of the mother country. The Puritan model in New England was the most severe, as the only entity the Pilgrims hated more than the princely world of the Anglican Church was the Church of Rome. The Virginia model was founded on the Established Church and tolerated no dissenters, such as the Pilgrims, but was equally forbidding of Catholics. Anti-Catholic disabilities were found in the legislation of every colonial statute, including Rhode Island, the colony generally seen as the "cradle of religious liberty." A 1664 law in Rhode Island specifically excepted Catholics from the right to public office. Maryland, a safe haven for Catholics when established in 1634, by 1694 had forbidden public Mass and established the general Catholic disabilities common to English law. William Penn attempted to begin his colony of Pennsylvania as a haven for freedom of religion, but within a short time laws were passed in the colony that forbade public Mass and denied public office to Catholics.

As the divisions between England and the colonies grew more severe in the eighteenth century, anti-Catholicism became more intense. The Quebec Act of 1774 — one of the Intolerable Acts of the English Parliament that strained relations with the colonies to the breaking point — roused anti-Catholic fever as it appeared to legalize a Catholic presence west of the Alleghenies. We have a "popish French government in our rears set up for the express purpose of destroying our liberties," a popular pamphlet proclaimed. During the Revolution itself, the new American government downplayed anti-Catholicism as it sought aid from the traditional Catholic enemies of England: France and Spain. Tory propaganda, however, was quick to play the anti-Catholic card and proclaimed that the Revolution meant that Boston's "Old South Meeting House is fitted up for a Cathedral, and that several other meeting-houses are soon to be repaired for convents."

The Catholic population after the Revolution numbered about twenty-five thousand out of a population of nearly three million. While most legal disabilities ended after the ratification of the Constitution, the nearly invisible — and primarily poor — Catholic population did little to dissuade the new America from its inherited anti-Catholic prejudices. By the time there was a new America, anti-Catholicism was one hundred sixty years old in the American consciousness and all the classic elements of this English heritage were in place. From the very beginning of the republic, Catholics were considered a foreign element that could undermine democracy. They had an allegiance to a faith intent on imposing its will on the American experiment. The Catholic faithful were seen as an ignorant, superstitious people who were satisfied with mindless ritual and had no understanding of the true tenets of their faith, for if they did, they would abandon it. Its leadership was anti-enlightenment and ruled tyrannically over its members, who were drawn from the inferior races of the world.

Historians of the American scene generally confine the recognized periods of anti-Catholicism to four general eras: the Philadelphia riots in the early 1840s followed by the Know-Nothing political movement in the late 1840s and 1850s; a brief flare-up in the 1890s with the American Patriotic Association; the Smith-Hoover presidential campaign of 1928; and a final curtain call during the presidential campaign of John F. Kennedy in 1960, after which it disappeared from the American scene completely.

The truth is much different. Anti-Catholicism has touched every period of American history. From our English heritage it is both ongoing and remarkably similar in its approach from era to era, including our own period of secular anti-Catholicism. Three anti-Catholic events in U.S. history, with broad impact on the popular culture, are noted below. All three are outside the traditional anti-Catholic periods that history usually details, and reflect the anti-Catholic assumptions held today.

Maria Monk and Popular Anti-Catholic Publishing

Anti-Catholicism had been a force in the United States since shortly after the last shots were fired in the Revolution. By the 1820s, a strong Protestant revival was under way and anti-Catholic newspapers were widely distributed. This was coupled with a change in immigrant patterns from Ireland, when Catholics from the South — rather than the Irish Protestants from the North in earlier years — began to arrive in growing numbers on the Atlantic coast. Books detailing convent horror stories became enormously popular in the United States in the 1830s. Most of these were imported from England. Works such as *Master Key to Popery, Female Convents,* and *Secrets of the Nunneries Exposed* established the common elements of anti-Catholic literature: lecherous priests, secret tunnels between seminaries and convents, and the babies who resulted from these unholy unions slaughtered and buried in basements.

The first distinctly American work to gain widespread popular attention was Rebecca Reed's *Six Months in a Convent,* published in 1835. Reed claimed to have been a nun who escaped an Ursuline convent in Charlestown. (The Mother Superior explained that Reed had not been a nun, but an employee who had been dismissed.) Reed's public telling of her story — prior to its publication — was part of the vicious anti-Catholic propaganda current in Boston that led directly to the burning of the convent by a mob on August 11, 1834.

There was not much to Reed's book, a first-person narrative rewritten by local Boston publishers who knew what would titillate the straitlaced Bostonians. Her story centered on various penances the nuns allegedly performed, none of which was particularly shocking or salacious, especially to modern readers. Still, this "inside story" would sell nearly two hundred thousand copies within a month of publication and remained in print for well over a century. Reed would not last long after her success. She died of consumption in 1838. Her supporters claimed that her death was caused by the harshness of her convent life. In any case, by the time of her death, Reed's book would be overwhelmed by the success of the most famous work of anti-Catholic literature ever distributed in America.

Awful Disclosures of the Hotel Dieu Nunnery of Montreal (or as it was more popularly known then — and now — *The Awful Disclosures of Maria Monk*) was first published in 1836. It would sell hundreds of thousands of copies in its early years and has continued to be published ever since. Born in Canada, Monk claimed in her *Awful Disclosures* that she was raised a good Protestant girl and entered the convent school at the Hotel Dieu in Montreal for her education. Impressed by the appearance of holiness in the sisters, she decided to convert to Catholicism and become a nun. Her mother told a different story. She claimed Maria's problems began when her daughter stuck a pencil into her head as a child. By the time Maria was a teen, her mother could no longer control her and had her committed to a Catholic asylum in Montreal. She said the girl had never been a Catholic and was never inside the Hotel Dieu.

According to Maria's version, after making her vows she was forcefully introduced to her main responsibilities as a nun: serving the perverse sexual needs of Catholic priests. She alleged that the babies that resulted from these unholy unions were killed. She claimed that she had discovered a gruesome cemetery in the convent's basement where the tiny bodies were buried, along with the young nuns who refused to take part in the orgies. Monk claimed that a "Father Phelan" had caused her pregnancy and, fearing the murder of her child, she fled the convent. That was where the first edition of the *Awful Disclosures* ended. In the second edition, the tale continued with attempted suicide, pursuit, and, finally, her arrival in the United States. She claimed to have been found, pregnant and near starvation, by hunters in the outskirts of New York. She told her terrible story to a Protestant clergyman who encouraged her to write it down.

The reality of the story was a bit different. Monk had taken off from the Catholic asylum to which her mother had committed her. She had help from her former lover, who was the likely father of her child. In New York, she hooked up with a few Protestant clergymen who saw the opportunity to make a strong anti-Catholic statement, as well as a few bucks. (It is claimed that the Rev. J. J. Slocum of New York was the actual author of the *Awful Disclosures*.) Those ministers approached the publishing house of Harper Brothers with Monk's story. The Harpers set up a dummy corporation to actually publish the book, unwilling to have their reputation sullied with a salacious tale not for polite ears. The book was released in January, 1836.

The *Awful Disclosures* was an immediate sensation. Hugely successful, it received rave reviews in the contemporary Protestant press and was cited as the first accurate depiction of convent life. The small Catholic community protested that it was a hoax. As the controversy grew, two Protestant clergymen went to Canada to inspect the Hotel Dieu. When they reported that it was nothing like Monk's description, they were accused of being Jesuits in disguise. When a prominent Protestant journalist investigated and denounced Monk as a fraud, he was charged with taking a bribe from the Jesuits.

Monk's behavior did not help her cause. She disappeared in August, 1837, only to resurface in Philadelphia claiming to have been kidnapped by priests. She had actually taken off under an assumed name with another man. While this indiscretion seemed to discredit her story, there were many Americans still willing to accept her "awful disclosures" as truth. In 1837, she published another book claiming that pregnant nuns from the United States and Canada lived on an island in the St. Lawrence River.

That book marked the end of her literary career. Lawsuits attempting to recover some of the profits from her earlier books publicly revealed much of the corruption behind the whole story. In 1838, she again became pregnant and claimed that it was a Catholic plot to discredit her. She married, but her drinking and loose living led her husband to abandon her. In 1849, she was arrested for pickpocketing at a house of prostitution. She died in prison a short time later. In 1874, Mrs. L. St. John Eckel published a book in which she claimed to be Monk's daughter from her last marriage. It gave a picture of Monk's last days as well as the story of Eckel's conversion to Catholicism.

There has never been a period when the *Awful Disclosures* has not been in print in the United States. It remains one of the most widely distributed "religious" titles of all time, selling untold millions for many publishers over more than a century and a half. Pornographic versions have been published, as well as more toned-down efforts for the sensitive. In 1996, a new hardcover edition was released, selling for thirty-five dollars.

Monk's tale combined many of the traditional aspects of anti-Catholicism, particularly the perversity of Catholic priests, the "alien" nature of the Catholic religion to the purity of the American experiment, the Church's tyranny over its members, the anti-democratic Catholic immigrants flooding our shores, and the Church's singular desire for power. In 1836, Lyman Beecher, the father of Harriet Beecher Stowe, would publish *The Plea for the West,* in which he claimed that there was a

Catholic conspiracy to take over the Mississippi valley. Samuel F. B. Morse, inventor of the first successful telegraph in the United States, shared this belief, claiming that Catholic royalty was flooding America with immigrants who would soon become an internal army under the pope's direction. It is said that Morse was not particularly an avid Protestant. When he was in Rome a papal guard knocked off his hat when he refused to remove it as the pope passed by. Thus, a lifelong animosity was born.

'The Menace' and the Anti-Catholic Press

Anti-Catholicism during the post-Civil War "Gilded Era" through the turn of the century was driven by the growing Catholic urban strength and the usual canards so popular in the American mind and not confined merely to the lower classes. "Prestigious journals like *Harper's Weekly* and *Atlantic Monthly* regularly featured anti-Catholic and anti-immigrant articles and cartoons. Just before the national election of 1884, a prominent supporter of Republican presidential candidate James G. Blaine denounced the Democrats as the party of 'rum, Romanism, and rebellion.' The slur was aimed at Irish Catholics, and probably cost Blaine the electoral votes of New York state and election to the presidency" (*American Catholics,* James J. Hennesey, S.J.).

The growing Catholic school system became a source for anti-Catholic rhetoric during this period. As the public school system was established throughout the United States, Catholic schools were viewed as a subversive counter-force indoctrinating immigrants in an alien faith. Catholic schools were also seen as a direct threat to the public school system. Any attempt by Catholics to secure a small part of the public funding for education was painted as an attempt by Rome to undermine America through subverting the public school system.

In 1876, the same James G. Blaine, as a congressman from Maine, introduced a constitutional amendment to prohibit the use of any public money for schools affiliated with churches. The measure was aimed at the Catholic school system. The measure passed in the House but fell short in the Senate. However, so-called "Blaine Amendments" became very popular and were enacted into many state constitutions, where they remain today. Thirty-one states presently have Blaine Amendments, or amendments derived from the Blaine formula, in their constitutions forbidding state aid to Catholic schools.

Anti-Catholic rhetoric as a debating tactic in current programs to allow public funds to be used in Catholic schools remains popular. There are legitimate arguments that can be aired on the issue, but most often the appeal is made to anti-Catholic sentiments. Catholic schools are still routinely portrayed as an alien presence in a community teaching un-American values. As an editorial in an Indiana newspaper proclaimed recently, the paper could never support the use of public funds "to teach papal infallibility."

In 1887, Henry F. Bowers founded the American Protective Association (APA) in Clinton, Iowa. An anti-Catholic, anti-immigrant populist movement in rural areas, the APA briefly achieved political prominence in the 1890s. "Members promised never to vote for a Catholic, never to hire one when a Protestant was available, and never to join Catholics in a strike. . . . It achieved its greatest prominence in 1893, when the A.P.A. spread the rumor that a papal decree had absolved all oaths of allegiance to the United States and that a massacre of heretics was planned for September 5, which they mistakenly thought was the feast day of St. Ignatius Loyola, founder of the Jesuit order" (*American Catholics*). The APA split apart in political and private schisms soon after, though it would still be active well into the 1920s. Its anti-Catholic rhetoric in the

1890s would find widespread appeal that would fuel the growth of a popular press dedicated solely to anti-Catholicism.

Thomas E. Watson of Georgia had founded *Tom Watson's Magazine* in the 1890s as a political magazine representing the Populist Party, a mixture of radical agrarian movements and urban labor. As the political movement faded and its circulation dwindled, Watson hit on a new means to attract subscribers. He published an editorial warning against "The Roman Catholic Hierarchy: The Deadliest Menace." For the next few years, nativist anti-Catholicism was the primary focus of his magazine and he was rewarded with growing circulation. (Watson would later become U.S. senator from Georgia in a career based on anti-Catholicism.)

A flood of anti-Catholic periodicals would soon appear on the American scene, all of which would be both profitable and widely circulated. A Commission on Religious Prejudices, established by the Knights of Columbus in 1914, counted over 60 such national weeklies with circulations ranging from 100,000 to 1,500,000 per issue. There was *The Campaign* in Boston, *Women's Witness* in Indiana, *The Converted Catholic* in Ohio, *The Patriot* in St. Louis, and *The Guardians of Liberty* in New York. The most successful, however, was *The Menace*, which took its name from the anti-Catholic editorial of *Tom Watson's Magazine*.

The Menace began out of an abandoned opera house in Aurora, Missouri, in 1911. Founded by Wilbur F. Phelps, the first issues were distributed for free, but within a short time it had a paid list of 120,000 subscribers. By 1914, circulation would exceed 1,400,000 weekly and be distributed throughout the United States. *The Menace* existed solely to attack the Church, and its pages were filled with convent horror stories, exposés by alleged former priests, ruthless Catholic assassination conspiracies, and columns of advertising promoting anti-

Catholic pamphlets and books, including of course the story of Maria Monk. The newspaper would be actively published until 1931.

The Menace regularly provided "Absolute Proof that Romanism Desired Death of Abraham Lincoln" and warned that Catholics were involved in poisoning President Warren G. Harding. Stories blamed the Vatican for instigating World War I and proclaimed that arms were being hoarded in Catholic churches in America for a planned uprising. "If we are going to have a Catholic Church," *The Menace* proclaimed in one issue, "let's have an all-American one. Let's not have one that makes foreign subjects of American citizens. Let's not have one that involves upon Americans the onus of kissing the toe of a big dago in Italy. Let's have one that does not involve political control of this country by a bunch of foreigners."

"What we are striving for," *The Menace* proclaimed, "is to EDUCATE THE PEOPLE of this republic of ours to a CLEARER UNDERSTANDING of the difference between allowing the Roman Catholic to worship God in his own way AND permitting the ROMAN CATHOLIC CHURCH, as a political factor, to put the Bible out of our public schools, elect her servants to office that the Church may prosper and the laws of the nation defied with impunity, and to say that the civil authorities cannot lawfully marry man and woman. . . . We are fighting the pernicious Roman Catholic doctrine of the infallibility of the pope and that the Church is the only proper agency for guiding the thoughts of our little ones, through its parochial schools, inculcating their impressionable minds with fallacious teachings. . . . Nobody ever got a dollar out of these tax-gatherers from the pope's garden and nobody ever will except assassins they hire to get presidents out of the way."

The Menace popularized an early bogus "oath" from sixteenth-century anti-Catholic literature. The Jesuits allegedly took the oath in early anti-Catholic works, but *The Menace* would attribute it to the Knights of Columbus. The phony Knights of Columbus oath would be popular in anti-Catholic literature in the 1920s and play a huge part in the 1928 election. It would be resurrected in 1960 in the campaign of Catholic John F. Kennedy. The oath had the Knights pledging to "make and wage relentless war against . . . all Protestants and to . . . rip up the stomachs and wombs of their women, and crush their infants' heads against the walls in order to annihilate their execrable race."

In April, 1914, Canada banned *The Menace* from its mail, which touched off a major debate in this country with organized Catholic demands that the paper be banned for libeling Catholics. The Knights of Columbus argued that libel laws should protect groups of people, not just specific individuals. (*The Menace* would be successfully sued by a Virginia priest whom the paper personally named, but the jury awarded him a paltry sum in return.) The attempt was made to ban *The Menace* under anti-obscenity laws (based on the publication's lurid tales from convent life), but this effort failed as well. Based on alleged reports in *The Menace,* bills were introduced in many state legislatures for "convent inspection" laws. These bills would allow inspectors to arrive unannounced and search convents for evidence of immoral behavior and unwilling enslavement of young women.

The distraction of World War I led to a decline in *The Menace* circulation. It dropped to about 250,000 circulation after the war and in 1919 its heavily insured building in Aurora went up in flames. (The suspicious insurance company refused to make a settlement, and *The Menace* would conduct a fundraising campaign in its pages to build a new home.) It would continue to actively publish, however, until it disappeared early in the Depression.

A major Catholic publishing house had its birth as a direct result of *The Menace*. Father John F. Noll, a pastor in Huntington, Indiana, had been involved in small Catholic publishing efforts since his ordination in 1898. In 1912, Father Noll reproduced two pages from *The Menace* and on the reverse side a Catholic response. He mailed this to every Catholic pastor in the United States asking the pastors to support a weekly newspaper that would respond to the kind of widespread popular anti-Catholic literature *The Menace* published. On May 5, 1912, the first issue of *Our Sunday Visitor* newspaper appeared and it would become the largest national Catholic weekly in the United States and one of the largest Catholic publishing houses in the world.

While World War I brought a respite from popular anti-Catholicism on a general level, it was during the war that the Ku Klux Klan was reborn. In 1915, William Joseph Simmons reconstituted the Klan as a secret Southern fraternal organization not unlike many such groups popular in the United States at the time. In the 1920s, the Klan would become a powerful political force with much of its public actions based on anti-black, anti-Semitic, and anti-Catholic activities. The Klan once again popularized the anti-Catholic lecture circuit and became a major distributor of anti-Catholic literature. Boycotts of Catholic businesses, laws to ban Catholic schools and Catholics from teaching in public schools — all of these things became a critical part of the popular Klan agenda. The Klan would tie up the 1924 Democratic convention and, in 1928, unleash a barrage of anti-Catholicism when the Democrats nominated Governor Al Smith of New York, the first Catholic presidential nominee.

Paul Blanshard and Secular Anti-Catholicism

The phenomenon of strictly nativist anti-Catholic publishing still exists in the United States. Enterprises such as Chick

Publishing in California distribute many of the classic anti-Catholic works as well as anti-Catholic pamphlets, comic books, and tapes. These can be found in many Christian bookstores today. The popular press, however, as well as mainstream secular publishing, still commonly produces anti-Catholic materials whose sources — and inherited prejudices — stem from Maria Monk, *The Menace,* and the revitalized Klan. Secular anti-Catholicism has been legitimate within American intellectual and academic circles for centuries and is considered normative today. One of the most popular writers in this vein produced his work just after World War II.

Paul Blanshard was born in 1892 in Ohio. The son of a minister, Blanshard was ordained a Congregationalist minister in 1917. He rather quickly abandoned the ministry, however, and renounced any allegiance to Christianity. He became caught up in labor work and the various aggressively secular movements popular among intellectuals of the time, including socialism and Margaret Sanger's crusade in regard to legalized birth control in which the Catholic Church was viewed as the primary enemy. In the 1930s, Blanshard allied himself with popular socialist agitator Norman Thomas and, while carefully distinguishing between socialism and Communism, argued for the end to what he saw as America's predatory capitalism. Blanshard soon broke off his flirtation with socialism and became involved in New York City politics, obtaining a city appointment when his candidate, Fiorello LaGuardia, was elected mayor in 1933. He developed a solid reputation for his investigation of official corruption. After leaving city government, Blanshard worked as a lawyer and, in World War II, served as a State Department analyst in the Caribbean.

Post-World War II Protestant America feared the growing public presence of Catholicism. Catholics were well represented in political circles and labor. Public campaigns that identified with the Church against indecent movies and literature, as well as in the growing anti-Communist movement, gave Catholics a prominence they never had before within American culture. "Catholic kitsch," as Charles R. Morris would call it in *American Catholic* (Times Books, 1997), "was spreading throughout popular culture" in the 1940s and 1950s. In a series of eight articles in the *Christian Century* toward the end of the war, editor Harold Fey argued that Catholicism was "winning America" by "mobilizing powerful forces to move this nation toward a cultural unity in which the Roman Catholic Church will be dominant." At the same time as Fey was issuing warnings from a Protestant perspective, the growing secular intellectual movement feared what they saw as a rising Catholic power that could allegedly control the content of movies, the banning of books, and the ballot box through sheer weight of growing numbers, particularly in urban America.

In 1947, Protestants and Other Americans United for the Separation of Church and State, or POAU, was founded by Methodist Bishop Bromley Oxnam. The POAU was part of what Father John Courtney Murray defined as the "new nativism," a highly secularist philosophy that viewed Catholicism as the enemy of America. The POAU and others would use anti-Catholicism as their primary tactic to attack aid to Catholic schools, the appointment of a U.S. ambassador to the Vatican, and to deny ordained Catholic clergy the right to vote as they were representatives of a foreign government, the Holy See. The POAU would find its leading public figure in Paul Blanshard.

Blanshard's antipathy to Catholicism began with his involvement in the birth control movement, but soon extended to the structure of the Church itself, as he saw it. Blanshard echoed centuries of anti-Catholic propaganda in his charge that the Catholic Church was an anti-democratic force bent on world domination, an alien power in American society determined to keep the masses poor, ignorant, and propagating. In March, 1949, Blanshard released the book *American Freedom and Catholic Power,* which would become the secular bible of an anti-Catholicism rooted in English anti-Catholic propaganda, but secular rather than Protestant in its arguments. In *Public Catholicism* (Macmillan, 1989) historian David O'Brien summarizes Blanshard's thesis:

> Blanshard contended that Catholics, if they became a majority, would be bound to seek three amendments to the Constitution, one recognizing Catholicism as the official religion, a second supporting Catholic education and requiring the teaching of Catholic morality in neutral schools, and a third imposing Catholic teachings on marriage, divorce, and birth control. Like so many earlier opponents of the Church, Blanshard attacked the hierarchy, not Catholics themselves. If Catholics "controlled their own church," he argued, "the Catholic problem would soon disappear because, in the atmosphere of American freedom, [Catholics] would adjust their church policies to American realities." From an American standpoint, he believed that "acceptance of any form of authoritarian control weakens the democratic spirit." And the Church was indeed undemocratic . . . , dictating to parents what should be taught, engaging in devotions designed to place responsibility for belief in the hierarchy and clergy, and sharply limiting intellectual freedom for its teachers, scholars, and people. No dissent was allowed. Such practices could not help but weaken American democracy and only fear of being charged with bigotry kept intelligent Ameri-

cans from facing the fact that the Catholic hierarchy used American freedom to systematically cultivate separation and intolerance.

Blanshard's book was in its sixth printing by August, 1949, and gave renewed legitimacy to an anti-Catholicism with an intellectual veneer. Blanshard, of course, was appealing to most of the nativist, inherited anti-Catholic sentiments: an alien religion that desired to undermine American freedoms; a hierarchy controlling Catholics who were truly ignorant of the real tenets of their faith; and an authoritarian religion imposing its antiquated views on modern society.

Essentially, Blanshard's enormously popular books would establish the tone of the secular anti-Catholicism so prevalent today and normative within press and media presentations of the Catholic Church. Much of Blanshard's critique of Catholicism would be the basis of reporting on the Church reflected in the results of the Center for Media and Public Affairs study in *Media Coverage of the Catholic Church,* which was released in 1993. The executive summary of that first report stated that in the secular media:

> The Church was overwhelmingly portrayed as an oppressive or authoritarian institution. Over the course of time, the Church was increasingly portrayed in this light. An institution that was usually described as conservative and oppressive was also presented more often than not as irrelevant. . . . In sum, the linguistic tone of news coverage has been generally (and increasingly) unfavorable to the Church. At every outlet, and during every time period, it was usually portrayed as an oppressive or authoritarian institution with little relevance to the modern world.

Blanshard believed that Catholic influence transformed religion into a political movement. In 1945, Fey wrote almost admirably from a Protestant perspective of an effective Catholic faith that was dynamically changing American culture. In 1949, Blanshard wrote menacingly — no pun intended — of a Catholicism that extended far beyond religion to become a power within America that planned to take active steps to subvert the meaning and intent of the Constitution. (Curiously, while Blanshard was popularizing this threat of American Catholic power, in Catholic circles in the United States the great debate was over a thesis presented by Monsignor John Tracy Ellis in 1955 that Catholicism in America was having no impact on intellectual life. Within Catholic circles, Ellis's article "American Catholics and the Intellectual Life" prompted, Charles Morris wrote, "an outpouring of soul-searching lectures, articles, and books deploring Catholic backwardness.")

Blanshard kept up his attacks on Catholicism throughout the 1950s and into the 1960s. In *Communism, Democracy and Catholic Power* (1951), Blanshard equated the style of Catholic leadership and authority to that of the Communist leadership in the Soviet Union under Joseph Stalin. His basic thesis was that Communism and Catholicism represented the greatest threats to American democracy. In 1953, he wrote a work on Ireland that framed the country as a Catholic theocracy dominated by Church authority. In 1962, he issued a study of Franco's Spain, where Catholicism is identified with a fascist remnant from World War II.

Blanshard continued on well after his literary output waned. He wrote a few more books of general interest in the area of Church-State relations as well as a biography, but did not produce any more vociferously anti-Catholic material. In later life, he was more interested in defending a rabid secularist approach to life that moved him more to the fringes of

American intellectual culture. He died in 1980 at the age of eighty-seven. Most of his works are still in print, and *American Freedom and Catholic Power* remains quite popular in various atheist and humanist circles.

IV

On November 4, 1997, Oregon voters overwhelmingly rejected an attempt to repeal the 1994 Death with Dignity act that had made Oregon the only state with legalized physician-assisted suicide. In the original campaign for the legalization of euthanasia, the law had passed by the slimmest of margins, 51 to 49 percent. In the 1997 referendum, the margin was nearly 20 percent. Post-election analysis attributed victory for the pro-euthanasia forces to anti-Catholicism. The Catholic Church, while accounting for only about 10 percent of the Oregon population, remains the largest religious denomination in a state that is predominantly unchurched. However, pro-suicide forces were able to present a picture of the Catholic Church as an outside influence determined to overthrow Oregon law.

In the campaign, the complicated public issue of physician-assisted suicide was addressed only marginally. Instead, pro-suicide forces targeted the Church as an irrelevant, outmoded, and foreign institution that was attempting to interfere with Oregonian affairs. The basic concept of the referendum campaign was not the difficulties with the 1994 statute, nor whether physician-assisted suicide was good public policy. Rather, the focus of the campaign became the Catholic Church. A "Don't Let 'Em Shove Their Religion Down Your Throat Committee" was established with the Catholic Church as the religion to be targeted. As noted by Ann Carey in a post-election analysis in *Our Sunday Visitor* newspaper, anti-Catholicism was a popular tactic in the predominantly secular Oregon culture.

For example, Carey cited a radio talk show in Portland where "the host and several callers agreed that the Catholic Church should be considered a 'foreign power' and thus prohibited from contributing to state campaigns," in reference to Catholic fund-raising efforts to repeal the 1994 law. (Outside funding for the pro-suicide forces was large, including a quarter-million-dollar donation from a New York businessman, as well as donations from out-of-state chapters of the Hemlock Society, a pro-suicide group. There were no backlash complaints of sinister "outside forces" concerning these donations.) Barbara Lee, leader of Oregon Right to Die and a public figure in the referendum campaign, referred to the Catholic Church, in words echoing *The Menace,* as "a political machine driven by dogma."

The pro-suicide forces in Oregon were merely following a strategy laid out in the 1960s and 1970s in the abortion debate: Do not discuss the issue, but depend on anti-Catholic rhetoric to carry the day. In many ways, the pro-suicide debate has mirrored earlier debates and their use of anti-Catholic rhetoric, particularly the abortion debate. Dr. Bernard Nathanson, a leader in the early days of the pro-abortion movement who changed his thinking on the issue, claimed that anti-Catholicism through attacks on the Catholic hierarchy was the most useful tactic decided upon early in pro-abortion propaganda. Seeing that debates concerning when life begins and the whole rather repugnant business of abortion would not generate strong support for legalized abortion, propagandists relied on the more comfortable picture of an alien, un-American Catholic Church hierarchy trying to force its morality on the rest of the country. It was a tactic that itself was drawn from the movement to popularize birth control in the first half of the twentieth century, and was central to Paul Blanshard's thesis. One did not have to debate the issue of abortion, but simply chant "Keep Your Rosaries Off My Ovaries."

The anti-Catholic culture in America remains a potent force, and those seeking favorable media treatment popularly use it. The anti-Catholic prejudice inherited from our English cultural ancestry is alive, appealing, and exploited in the public square. This is reflected in press coverage, particularly as the press — like the media in general — perceives a culture that is all-embracing, secular, and rational. Catholicism is viewed as a benighted, dangerous world view that should be kept off the streets and confined to the sacristy, much as *The Menace* wished for an "American Catholicism" that would not undermine American freedom. The assumed prejudice is that Catholicism — an "alien religion" — cannot and should not be allowed to have any real part in the continuing conversation of public debate as it represents an un-American view.

Former *Washington Post* ombudsman Richard Harwood readily acknowledged the secular assumptions of the press in a paper published in Our Sunday Visitor's 1993 book *Anti-Catholicism in the Media.* Commenting on the first study of anti-Catholicism in press coverage by the Center for Media and Public Affairs, Harwood noted that there "is no question that secular thought is the preferred body of thought within the media." Today's anti-Catholic secularism — the ancestor of post-Guy Fawkes England, Maria Monk, *The Menace,* and Paul Blanshard — is firmly rooted in the American experience. As the Center for Media and Public Affairs study affirms, the media create a negative caricature of the Church in American society There remains an unwillingness to allow the Church's views a hearing in the public conversation, and anti-Catholicism is used as a regular tool of argument and presentation in the press, both in news coverage and opinion-making. A tactic that would never be allowed with any other group is allowed toward Catholicism simply because of inherited prejudices that do not recognize that this is, in fact, bigotry. Anti-Catholicism, like institutionalized racism, is normative in the press — acceptable, useful, and understood to be the product of an enlightened mind rather than that of a nativist bigotry.

The pervasive problem in the press in regard to the Catholic Church is that the Church is routinely presented as alien, un-American, oppressive, puritanical, and a contrary and unacceptable public voice in the contemporary culture. The Church's views can be dismissed, not on their merits or lack thereof, but simply by their source, since the views of the Church are at odds with the prevailing secularism by which the press defines American culture. The Church represents greed, hypocrisy, the desire to oppress, and the urge to wield power. These are themes as old as Guy Fawkes and as persistent as published editions of Maria Monk.

The revised study on media coverage of the Catholic Church reflects both the changes and similarities in anti-Catholicism in the media from 1963 to 1998. While the issues might change, it is the application of anti-Catholic methods and strategies that does not change. We are still essentially dealing with a public attitude toward Catholicism that shares the same basic prejudices developed from Elizabethan propaganda in the late 1500s and early 1600s. Whether the driving concern is religious animosity, nativism, immigration, Church-State relations, the public schools, birth control, abortion, or the cultural revolution, the same anti-Catholic canards will be utilized because they are understood and consciously shared by most Americans from the blue-collar worker to the academic ivory tower, from the man on the street to newspaper offices.

In *Anti-Catholicism in the Media,* the study on media coverage of the Catholic Church reported on a number of analyses from news sources in three five-year blocks between 1964 and 1988. To briefly summarize the main points of that coverage, during that period coverage of the Catholic Church weighted heavily against whatever position the Church was taking. "Although the opinion breakdown varied from one issue to another, sources supporting the Church were in the minority on the broad range of debates involving sexual morality and Church authority that dominated the coverage."

Much of the coverage of the Catholic Church in the period of the original study focused on internal Church debate in the post-Vatican II upheavals, or how the Church encountered the vast changes in America resulting from the ill-defined "sexual revolution" that was taking place during that period. Coverage focused on birth control and abortion, clerical celibacy, the roles of women and minorities within the Church, the Church's response to internal dissent from Church teaching, and issues related to power.

Controversies were generally covered with political labels, resulting in a "long-running media drama that pitted a hidebound institutional hierarchy against reformers from within and without. The language used to describe the Church in media accounts reinforced this portrayal. The descriptive terms most frequently applied to the Church emphasized its conservative theology, authoritarian forms of control, and anachronistic approach to contemporary society."

In the early report, the Church's teachings on sexual morality formed the leading topic of conversation in the media, with most stories stressing disagreement and dissent. Members of the hierarchy were portrayed as old celibate men enforcing an outdated sexual code on laity and clergy generally in opposition to the Church's teaching. Power, rather than belief, was the focus of the debate, with the Church institution attempting to control the life of the laity as well as the moral code of all Americans. Issues such as clerical celibacy received little notice in the first report, as this was before the "pedophilia crisis" during which celibacy would be viewed as a causative factor.

Coverage on birth control eventually gave way to coverage on abortion. In the beginning of the debate after the legalization of abortion, the Church's position was presented in a rather straightforward fashion, though generally ignored. Coverage did not include debate within the Church on the issue, primarily because there was very little internal dissent. However, it was common to use anti-Catholic rhetoric to respond to the Catholic position. It was also common journalistic practice to identity persons taking a pro-life stand by religion if they were Catholic. Pro-abortion forces were never identified by religion, unless there was the "man bites dog" report of a Catholic espousing a pro-abortion position. Catholics for a Free Choice, a pro-abortion front group with virtually no dues-paying membership and funded primarily by other pro-abortion groups, has managed a two-decade life span in the news media through this "man bites dog" journalism.

Coverage of issues of Church authority and power dominated the immediate post-Vatican II years with opinion generally favoring a decentralized Church authority — a more "American model." "The 1970s saw a dramatic change . . . (where) (w)omen's rights and status became the major point of contention" and the Church was routinely and roundly attacked by secular sources. The 1980s saw heavy negative coverage of the Church in regard to its handling of internal matters of dissent. Also, "Church involvement in politics was always seen as an inappropriate threat to the separation of Church and State."

The first study concluded that the Church was portrayed in the media as a conservative, oppressive, and authoritarian institution trying to "enforce its traditions and decrees on a reluctant constituency." The old Catholicism was alive and well.

The new study covering 1994 through 1998 shows a number of marked changes in coverage of the Catholic Church in the media. Surprisingly, the study noted a distinct decline in overall coverage. It also noted a distinct decline in the diversity of issues that involved coverage of the Church. Birth control, of course, has disappeared as the media viewed that as a settled issue inside and outside of the Church. But also issues such as abortion, the treatment of doctrinal dissenters, and authority within the Church received less coverage. "Overall," however, "current Church teachings or practices received less support in the 1990s than they had in the previous decade."

News coverage in the last five years tended to focus on a few broad areas with "a concentrated focus on debate over the role of women in the Church. . . . The voices of internal dissent were increasingly replaced by those of external critics." The position of the Church on women's ordination received virtually no clearly defined support and was generally used as a means for those outside the Church to attack Catholicism as an oppressive institution. "During the current decade, debate coalesced around the role of women. . . . The media debate was sharply tilted in favor of change."

The role of women is a flash issue in American society, a defining issue like gay rights that separates the allegedly enlightened from the allegedly hidebound. It is not surprising, therefore, that the Church's teaching on women's ordination would be the main opportunity for anti-Catholic news coverage today.

V

The so-called "Sisters of Perpetual Indulgence" are a self-described street theater troupe of gays, transvestites, bisexuals, and lesbians in San Francisco. They dress in traditional nuns' habits and engage in vicious anti-Catholic activities. Calling themselves by names such as "Sister Missionary Position," they carried on vicious anti-Catholic protests during the papal visit to San Francisco in 1987, conducted an offensive Eucharistic parody called the "Condom Savior Mass," and held a contest for the "hunky Jesus" at a 1999 Easter event. The "Sisters of Perpetual Indulgence" are publicly and purposefully anti-Catholic and represent in their own unique way the continued prominence of anti-Catholicism as both a tactic to gain exposure and a successful means of expression in American society.

The "Sisters" applied for a public permit to celebrate twenty years of their nefarious activities on Easter Sunday, 1999. Initially they were denied a permit to march on Easter Sunday, but that decision was overruled by the San Francisco Board of Supervisors. (This was the same board that actively opposed traditional Easter sunrise services on public ground as a violation of the separation of Church and State.) The archdiocesan newspaper *Catholic San Francisco* wrote an editorial and ran a guest column blasting the board's decision and asked that the permit for the "Sisters" be moved to any day but Easter Sunday. When the supervisors agreed to reconsider their decision, anti-Catholic rhetoric was everywhere to be seen. The president of the San Francisco Board of Supervisors claimed that the Catholic Church through the archdiocese was engaging in a "jihad against gays and lesbians" and that Church protest was "all homophobic." Catholics were told that they "don't own Easter," while others agreed that the "Sisters" ridiculed Catholics, but that Catholics deserved it. The board of supervisors reconsidered its reconsideration and the "Sisters" were allowed their Easter Sunday performance.

September 18, 1998, New York, N.Y. — The "Weekend Section" of The New York Times found four plays advertised on the same page dealing with Catholicism. Their treatment of the Church ranged from ridicule to blasphemy. "Tony 'n' Tina's Wedding" features an Italian wedding in which a pregnant bride on drugs interacts with a drunken priest. "Nunsense A-Men" takes the antics of "Nunsense" — nuns use drugs and hawk a Blessed Virgin Mary cookbook that contains sexual innuendo — a step further, by having the characters in drag. "Late Nite Catechism" targets the pre-Vatican II Church. And "Corpus Christi" portrays Jesus having sex with his apostles. The page's theater advertisements contained not one production targeting any other religion. — 1998 Report on Anti-Catholicism, *Catholic League for Religious and Civil Rights*

Anti-Catholicism is the last refuge of acceptable bigotry in the United States. It is mainstream in the press, mainstream in the media, mainstream in American thought and culture. It has changed little since Guy Fawkes and his ill-fated co-conspirators were executed following their failed plot to kill the king in 1605 and the English began to burn the pope in effigy every November the fifth.

Robert Lockwood, former president of the publishing division of Our Sunday Visitor, Inc., is a graduate of Fairfield University with a degree in history. Lockwood was editor of *Our Sunday Visitor* newspaper for over a decade. He writes a biweekly column for *Our Sunday Visitor* newspaper and is a commentator for Catholic Family Radio.

CHAPTER ✧ 2

Pious Prejudice: Catholicism and the American Press Over Three Centuries

By Lou Baldwin

Anti-Catholicism, one of the few forms of bigotry socially acceptable in America, is quite possibly the nation's original sin. While not as vicious as racism, it is as American as apple pie and older than the Republic. Like so many recipes handed down from generation to generation, the modern, mass-produced, plastic-wrapped product lacks that certain zest and bite of the original, even if — in the case of bigotry — it is still difficult to stomach.

Take, for example, an item from the June 10-17, 1723, *New England Courant,* published in Boston by James Franklin, Benjamin Franklin's older brother: The pope "still complains of a Pain in his Foot, which undoubtedly affects his Toes: and we all know that the honour and Happiness of a great number of Catholicks depends upon the health of his Holiness's Great Toe, which by this Account, I am afraid is not in kissing Condition."

That was fairly mild compared to some of what went before in colonial America — before there was a Franklin, or even a newspaper for that matter. New England may have been the cradle of liberty, but it was also the cradle of American anti-Catholicism. Of course our Protestant forefathers would have considered that perfectly logical. Popery, they truly believed, was inconsistent with morality and liberty.

Consider an admonition from an early edition of the *New*

England Primer, the book from which generations of colonial children learned to read:

> Abhor the arrant Whore of Rome
> And all her blasphemies;
> And drink not of her cursed cup
> Obey not her decrees.

The papacy, the children were constantly warned, was "the whore of Babylon," the pope was "the man of sin," the Antichrist, the devil incarnate.

A number of such examples are cited by Sister M. Augustina Ray, in her 1936 *American Opinion of Roman Catholicism in the 18th Century,* probably the most thorough examination of colonial anti-Catholicism.

The January, 1746, issue of the Boston-published *American Magazine* informed its readers, "Popery is, by the invention of Commutations and Dispensations for the Breach of the Moral Law, the strongest enforcement of Vice, under the sanction of Religion; Protestantism, by placing Religion in the Practice of universal Virtue, as that Virtue is the Will of God, is the strongest enforcement of the moral Law."

Some of the greatest names in the pantheon of colonial and Revolutionary heroes were downright bigots when it came to the subject of Catholicism. For instance, patriot Samuel Adams, writing in the *Boston Gazette* on April 4, 1768, claims that "there is a variety of ways in which POPERY, the idolatry of Christians, may be introduced into America, which at present I shall not so much as hint at. . . . Yet, my dear countrymen, suffer me at this time to warn you all, as you value your precious civil liberty, and everything you call dear to you, to be on your guard against POPERY."

Paul Revere executed copies of anti-Catholic engravings

from the London press for reproduction in the *Royal American Magazine,* and in a ride somewhat longer than Boston to Lexington "on the 18th of April in '75," he rode from Boston to Philadelphia a year earlier to deliver to the Continental Congress the Suffolk Resolves, which had been disseminated throughout the New England press. Article 10 declared that "the late act of Parliament for establishing the Roman Catholic Religion and the French laws in that extensive country now called Canada, is dangerous in an extreme degree to the Protestant religion and to the civil rights and liberties of all Americans: and therefore as men and Protestant Christians, we are indispensibly obliged to take all proper measures for our security."

While anti-Catholicism appears to have been present in all of the English colonies, it seems to have been most virulent in New England, probably because that region was a stronghold of the Puritans, whose Low Church tenets made them suspicious not only of Catholics but also of Anglicans and any other denomination that retained traces of the Old Religion. Then, too, New England was in close proximity to Catholic Canada, a colony of France, the mother country's bitter enemy.

One would suppose this hatred of Catholics would have abated with the French and Indian War, which ended in victory for England. Quite the opposite.

The conquest of Canada presented a new situation. Here was a whole colony of Catholics, and under the peace treaty they would have certain rights. Toleration of Catholics, tacitly accepted in the Proclamation of 1763, was enshrined in law by the Quebec Act of 1774, which even permitted the Church to collect tithes. Needless to say, this infuriated the Protestant-dominated English colonies. Anti-Catholicism may not have been the prime cause of the American Revolution, but it most certainly was a contributing cause.

The *Newport Mercury,* in its August 27, 1774, issue, called the act "the only statute passed these two hundred years to establish Popery and arbitrary power in the British dominions."

The *Boston Gazette,* on October 17, 1774, reported that "Protestants in Quebec are obliged to practice their religion in secret in fear of offending Catholics."

Another Massachusetts paper, the *Boston Evening Post,* of September 17, had carried an interesting rumor datelined London: "It is reported that the Pope has been solicited to publish a Crusade against the rebellious Bostonians, to excite the Canadians, with the assistance of the British soldiery to extirpate these bitter enemies of the Romish religion and monarchial power."

The *Pennsylvania Gazette,* on September 28, had warned, "It remains to make the resemblance more complete, to introduce the inquisition at Quebec, and to erect Lord North's statue at Boston, in the posture of the Duke of Alva's at Antwerp, trampling upon the expiring liberties in America."

War, like politics, makes strange bedfellows. If ingrained anti-Catholicism had helped goad the fractious colonials into rebellion against the mother country, the realities of the conflict, when it came, drove them, where else? Straight into alliance with Catholic France and Spain.

Once the European alliances had been forged, the American press virtually ceased attacks on Catholicism.

The good, or at least tolerant, relations between Catholics and their Protestant neighbors forged during the Revolutionary War continued into the early years of the new nation. Catholics, after all, were still a tiny minority — less than one percent of the population of the thirteen founding states. The new federal constitution unequivocally provided equal rights to persons of all religions or no religion. While a majority of the new state constitutions contained clauses restricting the civil rights of Catholics, these were largely ignored but retained on the books because latent ingrained prejudice made them difficult to remove, in some cases until well into the nineteenth century.

As Catholic immigration increased, so did public anti-Catholicism. At first it was most apparent through the emerging Protestant church press. Early weeklies included the Presbyterians' Boston *Recorder,* the Baptists' *Christian Watchman,* and in New York *The Observer,* founded by brothers of telegraph inventor Samuel F. B. Morse (himself a lifelong Catholic-baiter and founder of New York's *Journal of Commerce*).

That Protestant denominational newspapers and journals should carry anti-Catholic material was almost a given, considering the confrontational spirit of interfaith relations at the time. Protestants would fare no better in Catholic newspapers, which rarely had a kind word for their separated brethren. The difference, like it or not, was that America really was a Protestant country at the time, no matter what the Constitution said. By 1827, there were no less than thirty Protestant newspapers in the United States, all united in one cause: a suspicion of Roman Catholicism.

By contrast, there were but three tiny Catholic newspapers: the *United States Catholic Miscellany,* published in Charleston, South Carolina; *The Truth Teller* in New York; and *The Jesuit,* published in Boston. Responding to the almost mystical powers for mischief and intrigue Protestants ascribed to the Society of Jesus, *The Jesuit* very soon changed its name to *The Boston Pilot.*

Indeed, anti-Catholicism was a unifying agent for the various denominations. As the nondenominational weekly *The Protestant* stated at the time of its founding in 1830, "The sole objects of this publication are to inculcate Gospel doctrines against Romish corruptions, to maintain the purity and sufficiency of the Holy Scriptures against Monkish traditions, to exemplify the watchful care of Immanuel over the 'Church of God' which he hath purchased with his own blood, and to defend that revealed truth, which Luther and Zwingli; Calvin and Arminius; Cranmer and Knox; Usher and Rutherford; Baxter and Owen; Burnett and Neal; Wall and Gale; Whitefield and Wesley, and all their different followers ex anima and una voce, have approved, against the creed of Pope Pius IV. . . ."

The weekly proved to be so viciously anti-Catholic that moderate Protestants turned against it, reasoning that its attacks could only create sympathy for Catholics.

The willingness of *The Protestant* to print any material against Catholicism, no matter how outlandish or absurd, was proven when Philadelphia's Father John Hughes (later Bishop and Archbishop of New York), under the pseudonym "Cranmer" submitted a series of letters to the newspaper outlining Popish designs on America.

After *The Protestant* swallowed the bait by printing the letters, Hughes publicized the deception in *The Truth Teller*.

Combating Protestant anti-Catholic propaganda played a major part in the establishment of the Catholic press, as *The Truth Teller*'s name would imply. In point of fact, Philadelphia's early Catholic newspaper, the *Catholic Herald,* was founded in 1833 primarily to serve as a platform for articles written by Hughes (with help from the scholarly Bishop Francis Kenrick) during public debate with John Breckenridge, secretary and general agent for the Presbyterian Church and a former chaplain to Congress. Breckenridge's side of the mutually harsh and abusive debate was printed in *The Presbyterian*. The acrimonious exchange via newspaper ended after about nine months with both sides claiming victory; notwithstanding each side's claim, a good result of the debate was the continuation of the *Catholic Herald* as a diocesan newspaper.

Philadelphia's public press was not particularly anti-Catholic. As a matter of fact, Mathew Carey, arguably the city's leading journalist, pamphleteer, and book publisher in the early nineteenth century, was an Irish-Catholic immigrant. While his sympathies lay with the trustees during the Church's struggle with trusteeism at that time — and he was essentially a secular writer — he remained a practicing Catholic and could be an ardent defender of the Church when it was under attack by outsiders. The same cannot be said for his descendants. Henry C. Lea, Carey's grandson, was the author of *The History of the Inquisition in Spain,* which, along with Lea's other works, has been providing ammunition for Catholic bashers since the nineteenth century.

The greatest single issue that preoccupied the Protestant press in the early years of the Republic was the Catholic plot to take over the United States, a fear fed by accelerating Catholic immigration and a proliferation of Catholic dioceses and parishes. The nativist anti-immigration movement was essentially anti-Catholic. Lesser issues that caused tempers to flare would revolve around the conduct of the public schools, which were virtually Protestant parochial schools, and a pathologically unhealthy fascination with the doings of religious sisters in Catholic convents.

An example of this that ended in violence centered on the Ursuline Convent School that had been established in Charleston, Massachusetts, in 1818. Many of the pupils were Protestant, something which did not sit well with the religious leadership. In the 1830s, Lyman Beecher, a Congregational minister and father of Harriet Beecher Stowe, preached a series of viciously anti-Catholic sermons that fanned the flames of bigotry, as did the publication of a number of pamphlets containing spurious accounts of supposed cruelty and immorality in the convents.

In July, 1834, one of the Ursuline nuns, Elizabeth Harrison, suffering from an apparent nervous breakdown, left the Ursuline convent and sought shelter at a neighboring home. Within a few days she changed her mind and, with Bishop Edward Fenwick's permission, returned to the Ursulines.

Rumors began to circulate that Miss Fenwick was being held in the convent against her will. Hearsay was given the stature of fact in an August 8 article in the *Boston Mercantile Journal,* which recounted the incident, adding that Miss Harrison had been persuaded to return, "being told if she would continue but three weeks longer, she would be dismissed with honor. At the end of that time, a few days since, her friends called for her, but she was not to be found, and much alarm has been excited in consequence."

The story was picked up and repeated by the *Morning Post* and the *Commercial Gazette,* and further inflamed by sermons by the likes of Lyman Beecher. On August 11, a mob burned the convent and school to the ground. Luckily, the sisters and their sixty pupils were able to escape through a back gate before the fire was started.

Quite naturally, this act of barbarism was universally denounced by the secular press and much of the religious press, blissfully unmindful of the role they themselves had played by fanning the flames of bigotry.

"Every Bostonian blushes for the conduct of those deluded men who set fire to the Ursuline convent," said the *Commercial Gazette,* which also complimented Bishop Fenwick for his efforts to persuade Catholics not to retaliate in kind.

The 1840s and 1850s saw the emergence of the anti-immigration movement — nativism, and its unlovely child, Know-Nothingism. The purpose of these movements was to limit immigration (translate that as Catholic immigration) into the United States, stiffen naturalization laws to the point where immigrants would not receive the franchise until they had twenty-one years' residence, and preserve American (read Protestant) institutions.

From a media standpoint, what is interesting is the emergence of a new genre of anti-Catholic publications; while sympathetic to Protestant ideals, they claimed to be political, rather than religious-based. The *Native American,* founded in Philadelphia in 1844, called for the extension of the period of naturalization and the election of none but native-born. In an oblique reference to Catholicism, it advocated the eradication of "foreign interference from all our institutions; social, religious and political." Other newspapers of a similar bent included the *Native Eagle and American Advocate,* the *National American,* and New York's *American Republican.*

The great issue for Catholics in the 1840s was opposition to Protestant influence in the public schools, notably through Bible reading and prayers and an anti-Catholic bias in textbooks.

New York's pugnacious Bishop Hughes was quite outspoken in defense of Catholic schoolchildren, but it was in Philadelphia where the mild-mannered Bishop Kenrick sought equal treatment for Catholics that matters came to a head.

It happened on May 6, 1844, when nativist American activists sought to hold a political rally in the district of Kensington, at the time a Philadelphia suburb. By chance or design, the rally found itself directly in front of the Hibernian Hose Company, an Irish Catholic volunteer fire company. During the general melee that inevitably followed, one of the young Protestant demonstrators was shot and killed. The nativist press had a field day. According to the accounts in the newspapers, the young man, George Shiffler, was carrying an American flag that was torn from his grasp and deliberately trampled by the brutal Irish mob.

The *Native American,* which said it had previously protested against making the nativist cause a religious one, now announced a change in position. "Another St. Bartholomew's day is begun on the streets of Philadelphia," the editor wrote. "The bloody hand of the Pope has stretched itself forth to our destruction. We now call upon our fellow citizens who regard free institutions, whether they be native or adopted, to arm. Our liberties are now to be fought for; let us not be slack in our preparations."

The editorial betrays more than was intended. It calls for fellow citizens, "native or adopted," to arm themselves. In plain words this is not opposition to foreign-born; it is opposition to foreign-born Catholics. As a matter of fact, the population of Kensington, where the riot occurred, was virtually entirely foreign-born — English and Scotch-Irish Protestant weavers fighting for turf rights with Irish-Catholic laborers.

The mixed ethnic and religious character of the riots was evident on May 8 when the Protestant mob burned predominantly Irish St. Michael's Church and hundreds of Irish houses in Kensington, then descended on the city proper to burn St. Augustine's, another Irish-Catholic church, bypassing St. Peter's, a German-Catholic church, along the way.

The educated classes, who controlled the daily newspapers in America and even the Protestant Church press and the nativist American press, expressed shock at these riots perpetrated by the ignorant underclass. But generally speaking, the daily newspapers accepted as truth the Protestant version of events: Church-burning is terrible, but those Catholics started the riots.

For instance, the *New York Herald Tribune,* reporting from a distance, editorialized on May 9 that "the source of the present excitement between the Irish and the Americans is to be traced to the politicians of both parties in this city and state aided and assisted by thoughtless priests." Further, "this state of things may be traced to ecclesiastics of this and other states who have deluded and used the poor Irish people here as the big beggarman O'Connell has done in Ireland. By attempting to govern political results as a distinct race or class, their conduct has aroused opposition of the whole American people of both parties, native as well as the naturalized of countries other than Ireland."

On the whole, even with biased reporting, the 1844 riots had the salubrious effect of placing nativism in temporary disfavor with the intelligentsia, the class that really controlled the mainstream press. It remained in relative dormancy until the 1850s when it reemerged as the political movement, Know-Nothingism, named for the secrecy surrounding its meetings and activities. For the most part the movement spread its anti-immigration, anti-Catholic propaganda, not through the general circulation newspapers, but through house organs, including *The Order of United Americans, American Republican, Native Eagle,* and *The Republic.* Strictly Protestant religious publications kept up a steady drumbeat of anti-Catholic articles through the decade. But most lucrative was the steady stream of viciously anti-Catholic books, which were so prolific, Ray Allen Billington wrote in *The Protestant Crusade* (Macmillan, 1938) that entire bookstores were devoted to such works. Former priests were favored authors, but the best-sellers were almost always "confessions" from former nuns, and usually, as was the case of the earlier Maria Monk book (see Chapter 1, pages 25-26 and 30-33), without a shred of truth. *The Convent's Doom, The Chronicles of Mount Benedict, The School Girls in France,* and *A Protestant Girl in a French Nunnery* were but a few titles of this lucrative genre.

Anti-Catholicism coupled with nativism was marketable. Nathaniel Currier, who founded Currier and Ives, played into the popular bias through an 1854 lithograph, "The Smile," which showed three stereotypically brutish-looking Irishmen happily drinking their beer. On the other hand, two decades later Currier and Ives would cater to the now more numerous and prosperous Irish Catholics through such colorful lithographs as depictions of an Irish religious pageant or the ceremony at which New York's Archbishop John McCloskey received his red hat. Such ceremonies, of course, did little to allay Protestant unease at the burgeoning Catholic population.

The Know-Nothing movement, which wrought great mischief on the fabric of American democracy, itself succumbed as a side casualty to a greater strife: the struggle against slavery and the Civil War. It tried to remain neutral on the slavery issue, an impossibility, given the passions of the times. In any case, with the advent of war, Catholics provided cannon fodder to both North and South, and in view of the national emergency, religious strife was again temporarily shelved.

Know-Nothingism's last white knight was Millard Fillmore, whose lackluster presidency (1850-1853) had contributed to the downfall of the Whig Party. As the 1856 Know-Nothing candidate, he stressed nationalism rather than anti-Catholicism, but received little encouragement from the public press. He ran a very distant third behind Democrat James Buchanan, the winner, and Republican John C. Fremont.

Long after its official demise, a vestige of nativism and Know-Nothingism remained through publications that continued after their founding organizations were no more. A prime example is *The Republic, a Monthly Magazine of American Literature, Politics and Art.* It had been founded by the Order of United Americans, a pre-Civil War nativist group, in its origins composed exclusively of native-born workingmen.

Under its gentrified form as a literary magazine, *The Republic* continued publishing for some years. As a point in fact, while one can find examples of what might be considered anti-Catholicism in newspapers throughout American history, this can be partly attributed to the sheer volume of material printed in newspapers. Relative to the number of articles printed, it would be difficult to make a case that most daily newspapers were anti-Catholic, although they might certainly have views in opposition to the Church on specific issues. Anti-Catholicism continued to be a staple in Protestant denominational organs, and in some secular magazines. It is much more noticeable in the magazines, which in certain cases played up to an anti-Catholic readership.

In some instances a particular magazine would have a steady diet of anti-Catholic articles for a period of its history but not at earlier or later times, something that probably reflected the bias of a particular editor or proprietor. The *North American Review*, easily one of the best American monthly magazines of the 1800s and early 1900s, printed an essay on "The True Lessons of Protestantism" in its March, 1882, issue. "I hardly need to argue that any revival of the methods of Catholicism could never occur except as the concomitant of a wholly improbable retrogression of society toward a barbaric type," wrote New England historian-philosopher John Fiske. "The very concept of an infallible church is so clearly a survival from primitive religious ideas, that to imagine such an institution presiding over the society of the future involves a most grotesque anachronism."

In other cases, an article with anti-Catholic bias would have to be viewed in the context of debate — the publication may have printed articles from a Catholic source with an opposite view. For example, the February, 1883, issue of the *North American Review* carried an article written by Bishop of Rochester Bernard J. McQuaid that took note of low church attendance by Protestants in comparison to Catholic church attendance. He wrote of past Protestant fidelity to "the inspiration of the Scripture, of a belief in God, the Father, Son and Holy Ghost, in eternal rewards and punishments," and other truths. He then warned, Catholics regret "in the impending struggle between infidelity and Catholicity, their aid shall be wanting and regret yet more that so many who were once members of Evangelical Church organizations shall be seen in the ranks, not of indifferentism, but of avowed atheism."

The reply two months later, by William Kirkus, "The Disintegration of Romanism," was somewhat less sugar-coated: "If Protestantism is decaying because of a diminution of its membership, which as a matter of fact, can be entirely disproved, a fortiori," Kirkus wrote, "must Romanism be decaying, which lost all Protestantism to begin with and is honeycombed with infidelity and groveling superstition?"

In the same spirit, the *North American Review,* in the November, 1889, issue, carried a debate entitled "Is Divorce Wrong?" The three essayists were Cardinal James Gibbons, Episcopal Bishop Henry Potter, and agnostic Robert Ingersoll. The almost predictable outcome suggests Bishop McQuaid had a point. Gibbons maintained divorce was wrong, Ingersoll disagreed, and Potter tried to straddle the fence.

Another *North American Review* article, published in February, 1890, on the papacy and its relationship with the kingdom of Italy had no such context of debate; it is pure bigotry. The writer, Gail Hamilton, in his article "The Pope and Italy" compared King Humbert of Italy to Leo XIII. "Humbert stands at the helm, watchful, graceful, constant, calm," Hamilton wrote. Leo "is borne along just as rapidly, but struggling, plunging, flinging against the current with vain and vociferous violence. No spoiled child hurls down his toy with more petulant willfulness than Leo XIII shows in thrusting back the fate which will not reinstate him to the Middle Ages."

While the occasional attacks on Catholics in the *North American Review* were by contributors and usually rebutted by other contributors, the intellectual weekly the *New Republic* assailed Catholicism editorially, often and viciously. In the September 2, 1916, issue, the editors declared: "The Roman Catholic Church has purposes to fulfill, has positions to maintain that seem incompatible with the progress of the community. It is the official propagandist of obscurantism. It stands four square against most efforts to advance scientific knowledge.

"The pope is sovereign of a state none the less real because it is unterritorial in character. He is aiming at a victory of certain principles conceived as ultimate and he is prepared to provoke conflict with all who come in conflict with his aims." But the *New Republic* assured its readers, "Just as what we term Prussianism contained, by reason of its very violence, the seeds of its own disintegration, so is this militant Catholicism destined to a similar destruction."

Herbert Croly was the editor of the *New Republic* at the time, and education guru John Dewey was a contributing editor. In the 1920s, persecution of Catholics in Mexico was an issue to American Catholics, who were urging the government to put pressure on the Mexican government.

Dewey, in an August 25, 1926, signed article, defended the actions of the Mexican government and said, "Propaganda by American Catholic laymen continues. We are glad to report the coolheadedness with which President Coolidge and Secretary Kellogg have refused to be stampeded and continue to set their faces against intervention in a situation which by every common sense interpretation of international law is a domestic one."

A curious editorial of August 10, 1939, revealed the *New Republic*'s somewhat misinformed idea of Catholicism. In a

Chicago parish bulletin, the *Voice of St. Sylvester,* a priest, Father Francis J. Connell, according to the *New Republic,* asserted that persons with venereal disease ought to be permitted to marry. The editor was aghast at this position, which was not politically correct at the time. The editor then went on to try to show Father Connell's alleged position was the official position of the Catholic Church. The newsletter, he argued, was too professionally written to be just a parish bulletin. Further, another article in the parish publication requested replies be sent to *The Catholic Family Monthly,* Huntington, Indiana. Huntington, the *New Republic* darkly informed its readership, "is a well-known center of Catholic publishing, being the home of *Our Sunday Visitor,* with a circulation of more than 450,000."

Church doctrine is unchanging; political correctness is not. One has to wonder, were Father Connell writing today and he substituted the word AIDS for venereal disease, would a liberal magazine disapprove if he argued persons with this modern sexually communicable scourge should be permitted to marry?

A November 11, 1937, article on persecution of Catholics in China and Spain included this gem: "It is true of course, that the elected government has shown no sympathy for the Catholic Church in Spain, where its record has probably been blacker than anywhere else in the world." In spite of this, the *New Republic* article paid Catholicism an unintended compliment. It was titled "The Church in Spain and China." No Protestant journal worth its salt would have conceded exclusivity to the Catholic faith by referring to it as "The Church."

The *American Mercury* was a more general, less intellectual magazine than the *New Republic,* but could at times be its equal in taking potshots at Catholics. Its February, 1935, issue employed a trick as old as nativism — using a renegade priest, in this case E. Boyd Barrett, a former English Jesuit, to vilify nuns. In the article "The Sociology of Nunneries," Barrett, writing of insights he claimed to have learned through hearing nuns' sacramental confessions, said, "The phenomenon is unique. In it there is an element of beauty as of tawdriness. In the nun's soul are twisted threads of love, nobility, bitterness and cruelty . . . the more she resembles an angel the less likely she is to be one. The most dovelike of them all is liable to be the most apt artist in inflicting pain."

A February, 1944, *American Mercury* article proved wars do not always mean a halt in religious attacks. J.H.J. Upham, president of Planned Parenthood of America, assailed Catholic Church opposition to the repeal of laws prohibiting contraception, saying that "this sort of activity by the Roman Catholic hierarchy is a direct and dangerous invasion of civil rights, as well as a startling infringement of the American principle of separation of Church and State."

A letter to the editor from Father John A. Ryan, president of the National Catholic Welfare Council, refuted Upham. He noted the bishops were seeking to keep existing laws that had been passed by mostly Protestant legislators. If Dr. Upham is correct, Ryan observed, then those legislators "must have been anti-democratic and un-American."

The venerable *Atlantic Monthly* published anti-Catholic screeds in fits and starts. For instance, the July, 1911, issue carried a critique of the process by which popes are selected, "Pontifex Maximus," by Guglielmo Ferrero. He likened it to the selection of the emperors of Rome, then said, "From Rome he still rules over interests and men scattered throughout the whole world, and the empire of which he is the head has the same constitution and is today affected by the same maladies which, even in its balmiest day, the Roman Empire was perpetually suffering."

Coming forward to the 1930s, there are several articles

that could only be described as anti-Catholic. In September, 1930, "Why I Should Find it Difficult to Become a Roman Catholic" was written by an Anglican churchman, Rev. William Orchard. The author professed belief in everything that Catholicism teaches from infallibility on down, even admitting he would have been content were he born Catholic, but then listed the many faults, real or imagined, of the Catholic Church.

January and February, 1928, saw articles by "Anonymous," a Catholic priest. The first was a criticism of priestly training. "The priest," Anonymous wrote, "submits humbly, abjectly, if he would maintain his standing. But many there are who rebel at heart. The world would be astounded to know the number of priests who are struggling with the desire to remain faithful to the forms of ecclesiasticism while their very beings cry against the system."

The second article, "The Heresy of the Parochial School," was an attack on the parochial school system. The Catholic Church in America, said Anonymous, "thwarts her own purpose by her education system. Like the Pharisees of old, the ecclesiastical authorities impose burdens on the people they themselves will not touch with a finger. . . . When the American bishops cease their school building crusade and begin to work on building Christian character, there will be hope for the Church in America."

Atlantic Monthly invited reader response, and a letter from Michael Williams, a Catholic layman, got to the heart of the matter. He wondered if it was mere coincidence that three leading magazines had anti-Catholic articles in their January, 1928, issue just as a Catholic candidate for president had emerged.

This is not the only instance where *Atlantic Monthly* allowed anti-Catholic writers to hide behind anonymity, something which made their allegations more difficult to disprove.

Another case in point was "The Road to Rome and Back Again" (April, 1932). A New England Protestant woman told of her conversion to Catholicism and her disenchantment (over birth control) with the Church.

Perhaps one of the most extraordinary pieces of equal-opportunity bigotry — against African Americans, Jews, and Catholics — to appear in a reputable magazine in the twentieth century was printed in the Spring, 1926, issue of the *North American Review.* "The Klan's Fight for Americanism" by Hiram Wesley Evans, Imperial Wizard of the Ku Klux Klan, spread its venom to its three favorite targets and in defense of "the Nordic Race," but in particular attacked Catholicism because of the increased influence of Catholics in the political arena. "The real indictment against the Roman Catholic Church," Evans wrote, "is that it is, fundamentally and irredeemably, in its leadership, in politics, in thought, and largely in membership, actually and actively alien, un-American and usually anti-American."

He went on to say: "We Americans see many evidences of Roman Catholic alienism. We believe that its official position and its dogma, its theocratic autocracy and its claim to full authority in temporal as well as spiritual matters all make it impossible for it as a church, or for its members, if they obey it, to cooperate in a free democracy in which Church and State have been separated."

Equal space was given in the Summer issue to four shorter articles on the Klan that had been written simultaneously, not in rebuttal. These were authored by Jesuit Father Martin Scott of the College of St. Francis, W.E.B. DuBois for the NAACP, Rabbi Emeritus Joseph Silverman of Princeton University, and Princeton Political Science Professor William Starr Myers.

The first three, as might be expected, roundly denounced the Ku Klux Klan and all its works. Myers's denunciation was somewhat milder. He saved his harshest criticism, not for the Klan, but for religious fundamentalism. "Any such movement therefore is even more opposed to the real American spirit than the racial and religious prejudice fostered by the Ku Klux Klan," Myers wrote in this early volley in the intellectual elite's emerging war against the Bible-centered foundations of Protestantism.

Myers's article was wide-ranging and idiosyncratic. Of greatest interest to Catholics would be his comments on the League of Nations and "the so-called World Court."

There is, Myers wrote, "widespread opposition to the nth degree with regard to the League of Nations due to the fact that both these world organizations are potentially, at least, under the control of the Latin and Catholic nations of Europe and Central and South America."

Myers's comment in the *North American Review* has enormous implications not only for America but also for the world. The American Catholic hierarchy had not been particularly sympathetic toward the League of Nations because of a perceived snub of Pope Benedict XV by staunch Presbyterian Woodrow Wilson, who refused to allow the Vatican to participate in the peace process.

Myers suggested Protestants were even more wary of the league because Catholic member-nations might outnumber Protestant member-nations (Africa and Asia were mostly spheres of influence for the European powers at this point in history).

If he is correct, the ultimate rejection of the League of Nations by the U.S. Senate was based on isolationism certainly, but an isolationism rooted in anti-Catholicism. Another world war would have to be fought before a viable international union of nations would emerge.

During the first half of the twentieth century, the secular

journal that most frequently published articles attacking the Catholic Church was the ultraliberal *Nation*. Negative articles attacking the Church were practically a department of the magazine unto themselves. A January, 1925, editorial against Boston's Cardinal William O'Connell's opposition to a child labor amendment said in part, "Whether one believes in the Amendment or is opposed to it, there can be no question that in mixing into this matter as he did the Cardinal did his church a great disservice. He thereby justified those who insist that the Catholic Church as such is active in politics and its aim is the domination of our political as well as our social life."

"Church Position on Birth Control" was an article written by Margaret Sanger and published on January 27, 1932. She wrote of the pope: "In that remote tower he sits comfortably, takes counsel from a pile of old books and from bachelor advisers and then writes scolding sermons about the marriage problems of intelligent people. I wish he could come down into real life for a few weeks and walk the earth and mingle with the poor 'Ye have always with you.' He would hear stories from Catholic, Protestant and Jewish women, which I think should be enough to shake some sense in any man."

That particular issue had no less than ten articles espousing liberal birth control policies. The *Nation* editorialized, "In America the chief enemy is, of course, the Catholic Church. That the opposition will in time be overcome, we do not question; there are too many Catholics themselves profiting by the knowledge of birth control, especially among the rich members of the church to leave any doubt of that."

Another editorial comment on February 25, 1931, belittled a pioneering radio broadcast by the pope to the world, which was arranged by inventor Guglielmo Marconi. "It is evident, the editors wrote, "the Pope is using his new freedom from the Vatican, his new dignity as sovereign of a state, to extend his power, to widen his influence. There will be plenty of persons who will watch with alarm any attempt to augment the enormous authority of the Catholic church, and in an age when Protestantism is at its weakest and wateriest, there may be cause for their fears."

The *Nation* played the former-Catholic card in a vicious two-parter written by novelist James T. Farrell and published on October 17 and October 24, 1936. "Down through the ages the Roman Catholic Church has balanced prayer with the rack," Farrell wrote, "canonization with the might of the sword, the power of wealth and oppression with the dreams and ignorance of the masses."

The *Nation* may have overreached itself in a series of articles that ran November 1, 8, and 15, 1947, and picked up again April 10 through June 5, 1948. These were written by Catholic-basher Paul Blanshard and were later reprinted in book form as *American Democracy and Catholic Power.* The articles — which began with "Church Control vs. Birth Control" and continued with "The Roman Catholic Church in Medicine," "Sexual Code and the Catholic Church," "The Roman Catholic Church and the Schools," "The Roman Catholic Church and Fascism," "The Catholic Church as Censor," and "The Catholic Church and Democracy" — were so biased that first, after Catholic complaints, the Newark public schools banned the magazine from school libraries. In June, 1948, the New York City public schools followed suit.

The *Nation,* in its July 3 issue, expressed shock; it had not been surprised by the action in heavily Catholic Newark, but in liberal New York City, where Blanshard had served as a commissioner of accounts when Fiorello LaGuardia was mayor, that was another matter. "We are dead-sure," the editors wrote, "it was the pressure of the Roman Catholic church that brought about the high-handed action of the board of superintendents.

We believe the church is today the most potent organized force opposing freedom and progress in this country."

"New York took a step backward toward the Middle Ages last week," editorialized the *New Republic*. "Its board of education, by a unanimous vote of the four members present, upheld an earlier action of the nine-member board of superintendents and banned the *Nation* from all public school libraries. . . . There was no attempt to conceal the fact that the ban was imposed because of pressure from the Catholic Church. A member of the Board of Education, George Timone, who acted as a Catholic spokesman, launched a violent attack on two series of articles written by Paul Blanshard."

The New York Times reported on the ban on Thursday, June 24. The story, which began below the fold on page one and continued on an interior page, was straightforward. It quoted from a statement issued by the office of William Janson, the superintendent of schools, which said, "The Blanshard articles have contributed to religious animosity by going into matters of faith and out of the realm of politics or social controversy. The series of articles by Mr. Blanshard are definitely anti-Catholic."

A school board member who opposed the ban, Maximilian Moss, said the ban "violated the spirit of the constitutional provision for the freedom of the press." There was also a statement from Freda Kirchway, the editor of the *Nation,* condemning the ban and another in support of it by Jesuit Father Harold C. Gardner, the editor of *America,* who said the *Nation* articles were "to say the least inadequate and inaccurate." He contended that schools, by carrying the magazine, gave tacit approval of its content.

The *Times* also reported on a telegram signed jointly by the American Civil Liberties Union, the Public Education Association, the United Parents Associations, and the American

Jewish Congress, which called the ban "a shocking and arbitrary act of censorship."

On the whole, the June 24 *Times* article was well balanced, with perhaps slightly more ink given to those opposed to the ban. A follow-up article on Sunday, June 27, was another matter. The page 34 article ran to four columns under a headline, "Blanshard Scores Church Censors." While the article did make note of the fact that Dr. Janson was Lutheran, about 80 percent of the article was devoted to Blanshard and his followers.

The New York Times offered no editorial comment on the ban — the bigger issue at the time was the nomination of former New York Governor Thomas Dewey as Republican candidate for president of the United States. During the same week there were several *Times* articles that presented the Catholic Church in either a favorable or neutral light. These concerned a new bishop and articles about Catholic persecution in areas under Communist control.

This coverage is rather typical of a national trend in the reporting of issues concerning the Church. In noncontroversial areas the coverage tended (and tends) to be friendly or neutral. However, in areas where the Catholic position might be disputed by others, especially the intellectual elite, coverage was less friendly.

While some secular magazines had a history of articles that could be considered anti-Catholic for at least a period of their existence (possibly under a biased editor), others did not. It would be very difficult to detect a pattern of bias in *Life, Look, Reader's Digest,* or *The Saturday Evening Post.*

Literary Digest, one of the most popular magazines in the first half of the twentieth century, did indeed print a number of articles that had an anti-Catholic bias. But on closer examination, these were usually done in the spirit of debate.

The magazine would seek out issues of controversy and run articles pro and con, then let the reader decide the truth. An example would be the May 24, 1924, issue that discussed "The Problems of a Catholic Candidacy." The candidacy in question was a possible run for the White House by New York's Governor Al Smith.

The pro side was reprinted from an article by Father Paul J. Blakely in *America* magazine. Blakely pointed to the careers of U.S. Chief Justices Roger Taney and Edward Douglass White as proof positive that Catholics could serve in high office with no damage to the Constitution.

The opposing view was reprinted from the *New Republic,* and it advanced the rather interesting theory that a Smith candidacy would pit the (Protestant) countryside against the Catholic-dominated cities and thus paralyze the country, which, the *New Republic* advised, should be united "against predation and arbitrary capitalistic control of resources of the nation. It is not the time to drag in the religious issue." It suggested Governor Smith would probably realize this and withdraw his candidacy before the Democratic convention.

The Catholic candidacy issue was still alive in May, 1927, when *Atlantic Monthly* published a letter submitted by Charles Clinton Marshall, a prominent New York lawyer and Episcopalian. There was, he warned "an irreconcilable difference" between the root principles of Roman Catholicism and the American democratic state.

While this persistent undercurrent of anti-Catholicism clearly played a role in the 1928 election, it is less certain that it affected the eventual outcome: At that point in Republican ascendancy only two Democrats had been elected to the presidency since the 1860 election of Abraham Lincoln.

The newsmagazines — *Time, Newsweek, U.S. News & World Report* — might have on occasion an article that could offend some, even many, Catholics. It was not a trend, but perhaps something inevitable given the controversial nature of issues covered, representative of a legitimate difference of opinion. There were, and are, many, many neutral or favorable articles in the newsmagazines that involve the Church.

Unquestionably, the high watermark in relations between the Catholic Church and the American press — be it newspapers, magazines, or church journals — was the era of Vatican Council II and the years immediately following. Publications that had rarely printed a kind word about the Catholic Church began to see it in a new light.

In the spirit of conciliar euphoria, *Atlantic Monthly* devoted its entire August, 1962, issue to a symposium on "The Roman Catholic Church in America." Protestant and Catholic contributors included Reinhold Niebuhr, Father Gustave Weigel, Barbara Ward, Robert Cross, and Monsignor Francis Lally. While some of the writers posed searching questions, none reflected outright hostility to Catholicism.

If John XXIII is ever to be canonized, one of the factors to be considered is the enormous strides made in ecumenical and interfaith relations through the workings of his council. In previous eras, the rise of Catholics and their aspiration to civil power had caused increased outbreaks of anti-Catholicism in America, outbreaks that were reflected in the media. This was true to a degree during the 1960 presidential campaign of the charismatic John Fitzgerald Kennedy. In fairness to the secular press, it was more often reporting the facts of the campaign, not stirring up passions. Resistance to a Catholic presidential candidate was most noticeable in the Protestant church press.

Christianity Today, in an October 24, 1960, editorial on the election, criticized "irresponsible and exaggerated hate charges not to mention false hate literature including the Bogus Knights of Columbus Oath." It then said, "Another barrier to a responsible airing of the religious issue has been the silence of the Roman Catholic hierarchy. As of mid-October there has not been as much as an official admonition to Roman Catholics that they disregard religious motivations in voting."

The same issue reported on a poll taken by the magazine of Protestant ministers — 3,062 respondents expected to vote for Richard Nixon, only fifty-five expected to vote for Kennedy. One wonders why *Christianity Today* was not calling upon Protestants "to disregard religious motivations in voting."

The Christian Herald, one of Protestantism's most influential monthlies, had printed editorials generally negative to Catholicism in its April, May, September, and October issues, all signed by Dr. Daniel Poling, the editor. The September issue also carried a full-page ad by Protestants and Others United for the Separation of Church and State (POAU), which severely criticized Catholicism.

Poling's November editorial was somewhat softer and took note of a backlash to the anti-Catholicism that had surfaced during the race. "This anti-bigotry campaign," Poling fretted, "would label all Protestants who do not vote for Kennedy [as] bigots." On the other hand, *Christian Century,* another nondenominational Protestant journal, was scrupulously fair throughout the campaign. It, too, accepted the POAU ad, but in editorial comment it was evenhanded. Coupled with worries about Catholic "bloc voting" were exhortations to all parties to consider religion as only one issue among many and to vote for a candidate, not a creed.

Ultimately the campaign would contribute to an at least temporary easing of religious prejudice. Perhaps it was Kennedy's — from a Catholic point of view — almost too abject declaration on September 13, 1960, to a ministers' group in Texas that his belief in separation of Church and State was absolute, and should there be a conflict between his conscience and the Constitution, he would resign the presidency. At any rate his televised speech played well in the press.

Kennedy's speech before the ministers was a timely counter to a September 7 Washington, D.C., meeting of one hundred fifty Protestant ministers and laymen that had also been widely reported in the press. The group, which was chaired by Dr. Norman Vincent Peale, one of the best-known American Protestant clerics and religious writers of his time, called itself "The National Conference of Citizens for Religious Freedom." *The New York Times,* reporting on September 10, said the meeting "produced a statement questioning whether Senator John F. Kennedy, if elected president would be able to withstand completely 'the determined efforts of the hierarchy' of the Roman Catholic Church to 'breach the wall of separation of Church and State.' "

While the *Times* report ran on an inside page, there had been a front-page report of a Jewish protest against the ministers' statement. The *Times* would ultimately endorse Kennedy for the presidency. "The statement of the Peale group with its myopic concentration on one issue is a disservice to Protestantism," *Christian Century* said. As for Kennedy's speech in Texas, it observed, "It is difficult to see how a Roman Catholic could have gone further and said more and remained a member of that Church."

Protestants and Others United for the Separation of Church and State, the group that had been most active in fomenting anti-Catholicism bigotry during the Kennedy campaign, traces its beginnings to another meeting of Protestant leaders at Chicago's Methodist Temple on November 20, 1947. Among the issues that brought them together, according to the group's magazine, *Church and State* (November, 1997), was President Harry Truman's proposal to establish diplomatic relations with the Vatican and Catholic efforts to obtain for parochial schools a share of government education funding.

Virtually every major Protestant denomination was represented at the Chicago meeting — Louie D. Newton, president of the American Baptist Convention; John A. Mackay, president of Princeton Theological Seminary; Methodist Bishop G. Bromley Oxnam; Episcopal Bishop William A. Scarlett; Carl A. Lundquist, representing the Lutheran Council; Frank A. Yost, representing Seventh Day Adventists; and Clyde W. Taylor, representing the National Association of Evangelicals.

There were also a number of educators, a representative of the Scottish Rite Masons, and an officer of the National Education Association, the nation's largest public schoolteachers' union. "Congress and all State legislatures," the group's manifesto said, "and all executive and judicial agencies of government must be warned that they are playing with fire when they play into the hands of any church which seeks, at any point, however marginal, to breach the wall that sharply separates church and state in this country."

The further history of Protestants United (which now claims fifty thousand to sixty thousand members) is an accurate illustration of the direction antireligious rhetoric has taken in America. At its foundation, according to *Church and State,* it was "a curious combination of liberals and fundamentalists, of Council of Churches and national and fraternal leaders."

It was an uneasy coalition. The word "Protestant" was dropped from the title in 1972. Henceforth it would be Americans United for Separation of Church and State. Americans United completely divorced itself from the fundamentalists who assisted in its foundation and who were, ironically, that remnant of American society that most closely reflected the religious beliefs of the colonial and Federalist Protestant founders of the nation.

An examination of *Church and State* issues covering the years 1997-1999 shows attacks on the Catholic Church continue, especially on issues revolving around aid to nonpublic schools, abortion, and Church participation in the public arena. However, the majority of the *Church and State* articles are directed against conservative Protestantism, touching on matters such as the posting of the Ten Commandments in schools or public buildings, prayer in public schools, the Christian Coalition, Pat Robertson, and Promise Keepers. The foe is no longer Catholicism alone — it is any form of Christianity, or religion for that matter, which is unwilling to compromise fundamental beliefs to conform to the secular humanism of the intellectual elite.

Not that attacks against Catholicism have discontinued. Such attacks, when they occur in the secular press, are usually triggered by opposition to a particular position of the Church rather than the Church itself. It could be a political cartoon against school choice every bit as nasty as the most anti-Catholic of Thomas Nast's drawings for *Harper's Weekly* in the nineteenth century. It could be a slanted opinion column, news story, or editorial. On rare occasions, the press shows bias through the advertising it accepts or rejects.

An instance of this was evident in *The New York Times* in 1995. On January 5 of that year, against the background of the killing of an abortion clinic doctor, Planned Parenthood ran a full-page ad in the *Times* that said in part, Catholic leaders "incite terrorism and violence" by their words against abortion. It named Cardinals John J. O'Connor of New York, Bernard F. Law of Boston, and Roger M. Mahoney of Los Angeles among "leaders of the anti-choice movement who have become the arms merchants in this war of words."

No one questioned the *Times*'s right to print the ad, but when the National Conference of Catholic Bishops attempted to counter with an ad of its own, it was a very different story. The controversy, which received national publicity through a Catholic News Service report, began when the *Times* received copy for the bishops' ad. Paid for by the Knights of Columbus at a cost of $69,000, it was headlined "Truth Doesn't Kill, Abortion Does." It quoted several statements by backers of abortion that admitted abortion does indeed kill babies, one of them taken directly from a 1963 Planned Parenthood pamphlet.

Before the ad could be accepted, the *Times* told the Pro-Life Office, it must sign a document agreeing to indemnify the newspaper if the ad resulted in a lawsuit. Further, it requested proof that everyone named in the ad had given permission for his or her name to be used. When the bishops' group asked if Planned Parenthood had been required to sign an indemnification agreement, the *Times* wouldn't say. Nor would it say whether or not Planned Parenthood had been required to seek permission from the cardinals named in its ad for the use of their names. In fact, none of them had been contacted. Only after adverse publicity and the bishops' group providing documentation for every quote did the *Times* back down. As it was, the bishops' ad was not permitted to identify one of the men quoted as "an abortionist." Instead he was described as a "director, Boulder Abortion Clinic in Colorado."

Rarely are slurs against the Catholic Church in modern newspapers as direct as an opinion piece by editorial writer David Boldt in the *Philadelphia Inquirer* on July 1, 1990. Boldt took issue with what he saw as Catholic attempts to influence the abortion debate. He wrote: "The Roman Catholic Church, it needs to be remembered, is quite literally an un-American institution. It is not democratic. The Church's view on due process and the status of women, to name a couple of key issues, is at odds with those that inform the laws of American secular society and its principal policies are established by the Vatican in Rome." Boldt later apologized for his perhaps hastily written opinion piece, one that was reminiscent of the writings of native-born Americans in the middle of the nineteenth century.

A most recent but just as blatant example of anti-Catholic bigotry appeared in the April 26, 1999, issue of *Time* magazine. In a generally negative report on school choice in Cleveland, writer Adam Cohen asserted, "Metro Catholic Parish School teaches many aspects of the nation's shared civic culture. But what it cannot convey is the American notion that all faiths and creeds are entitled to equal respect. The teachings of Christ infuse the academic environment. Hallways are lined with posters asking, What would Jesus do?"

If American anti-Catholicism is both historic and ongoing, as shown by the written record of the secular and religious press, it has had little adverse effect on the Church itself. Catholicism has flourished in America in the past three centuries as in few other places on the globe. Perhaps, as is the case with most religions, opposition makes the Church all the stronger. At times, it may even win converts, if not to its creed, at least to a better understanding of its place in America.

David Boldt, the *Philadelphia Inquirer* editorialist who had written so sweeping an indictment of Catholicism in 1990, has quite a different view today.

Another opinion piece written by him on June 15, 1999, addressed the issue of the fight for school choice legislation. Boldt cited several incidents of anti-Catholicism that had surfaced, including a comment by an Easton, Pennsylvania, teachers' union president who said, "If the Catholic Church were to disappear today, it would be better for all of us."

"It has been said," Boldt wrote, "that anti-Catholicism is the anti-Semitism of the liberal intellectual. And, as anyone who has dealt with the issue learns, anti-Catholicism runs like a river beneath the public debate on school choice, inside and outside legislatures. In my own discussions on school choice, I have often got responses like, 'I just don't want Catholics to get all that money,' spoken without a hint of the implicit bigotry."

Boldt is quite correct, even if with the passage of three centuries the face of anti-Catholicism has changed. The Catholic-baiters of today are rarely militant Protestants; they are almost always militant secularists. The words of Bishop Bernard McQuaid, written in 1883 in the *North American Review*, have an eerie ring of truth. It is Christianity itself, not just Catholicism that is under attack, and as the good bishop predicted, "In the impending struggle between infidelity and Catholicity so many who were once members of Evangelical Church organizations shall be seen not in the ranks of indifferentism but of avowed atheism."

Lou Baldwin is a staff writer for *The Catholic Standard & Times,* the newspaper of the Archdiocese of Philadelphia. He has written extensively on American Catholic history and is the author of *A Call to Sanctity* (1988), a biography of Blessed Katharine Drexel.

CHAPTER ✧ 3

Anti-Catholicism Today

BY RICK HINSHAW

Anti-Catholicism is deeply embedded in the fabric of America — so much so that Harvard historian Arthur Schlesinger, Sr., once termed it "the deepest bias in the history of the American people."

Historically, that anti-Catholic bias came from rather predictable sources of bigotry: hate groups like the Ku Klux Klan, anti-immigrant nativists, and hard-line anti-Catholic fundamentalists.

Today, however, an intensified anti-Catholic bias permeates American society — and it emanates not from these traditional sources of bigotry, but from cultural elitists who consider themselves paragons of tolerance. For major segments of academia, news and entertainment media, the arts community, the business world, and even government — all of whom would recoil in horror at the very notion that they are even capable of any form of prejudice — anti-Catholicism has become the last respectable bias.

Not a day goes by that the Catholic League is not confronted by ridicule of Catholic practices, defamation of that which Catholics hold sacred, and even blatant challenges to the basic rights of Catholics in America. Moreover — even as social pressures and government regulations are aggressively employed to extinguish other expressions of hate — anti-Catholic bigotry is defended and even celebrated as a legitimate exercise of free speech.

Why, at a time of such heightened awareness of the need for tolerance and diversity, does anti-Catholicism not only survive but also flourish in American society? And why is it particularly pervasive among our supposedly enlightened cultural elite?

The answer can be put succinctly in two words: cultural values. Catholic teaching calls the Church and individual Catholics to active engagement of the culture. As the National Conference of Catholic Bishops said in its document of November, 1998, *Living the Gospel of Life: A Challenge to American Catholics,* "The application of Gospel values to real situations is an essential work of the Christian community."

Today, the teachings of the Church have much to contribute in addressing the broad range of social problems that confront us as a society.

To cite an example, Catholic teaching on the sanctity of human life could, if widely understood and accepted, spur positive, life-affirming alternatives to all the manifestations of the culture of death: abortion, euthanasia, war, economic deprivation, violent crime and punishment, to name just a few.

Adherence to the Church's teachings on the paramount importance of the family could go a long way toward alleviating so much of the negative backwash of family breakdown — especially its devastating impact on young people, which so often manifests itself in such social pathologies as teen violence, substance abuse, sexual promiscuity, and out-of-wedlock pregnancy.

Similarly, an appreciation for the Church's teachings on sexual morality would do much to ameliorate the wide range of social crises spawned by sexual license: the AIDS epidemic, soaring rates of out-of-wedlock pregnancy, rampant abortion, and crimes of sexual violence, sexual abuse, and sexual harassment. Indeed, were Americans and our leaders versed in and committed to Catholic teachings on sexual morality, the nation might have been spared the terrible national scandal and resultant impeachment ordeal of 1998-1999.

On issues of social justice as well, the Church's teachings on the innate goodness and worth of every human being — so beautifully modeled in modern times by the late Mother Teresa's unflagging commitment to serving "the poorest of the poor" — could do much to inspire a spirit of true generosity to those in need; a giving not just from our surplus but from our substance, as called for by Pope John Paul II.

Yet, even as these teachings of the Catholic Church offer real answers to so many of our social problems, they are consistently met with hostility by the influential of modern society. The reason is simple: The Church's answers demand sacrifice, self-restraint, and personal responsibility — all of which are anathema to a cultural elite steeped in selfishness, materialism, and sexual hedonism.

Members of this elite recognize many of the same problems, but they want painless solutions that demand nothing of them: no change in their lifestyles, no sacrifices, no restraint of their material and physical appetites, and certainly no attribution of personal responsibility for the consequences of one's actions.

In this world view, abortion and birth control — rather than sexual restraint — become the ideal responses to out-of-wedlock pregnancy. Abortion also serves as an instant solution to poverty, disability, and child abuse, destroying the victims of these social problems and thus eliminating the need to sacrifice our own material desires in order to help care for them. Euthanasia and assisted suicide serve the same purpose: To eliminate the health care needs of the elderly, the terminally ill, and the disabled, you simply eliminate the elderly, the terminally ill, and the disabled. Condoms, rather than self-restraint, become the instant solution to the AIDS epidemic, and the disintegration of the family is enabled, rather than countered, by attacks on marriage and the transfer of parental rights and responsibilities to the public sector.

The Catholic Church stands, in the words of Pope John Paul II, as a "sign of contradiction" to these transient values of our secular age. In doing so, the Church not only contradicts those values, it also serves as a constant reminder of their emptiness.

The cultural elitists don't want to hear such reminders, because to do so would force them to confront the shallowness of their own lifestyles, and to contemplate the self-sacrifice and self-restraint that so terrifies them (even though, if they tried it, they might finally find the true source of the happiness and inner peace that all of their worldly pleasures and acquisitions have not delivered). So they do not just differ with the Catholic Church; they fear and bitterly resent its teachings, and are thus determined to stifle the Church's voice and negate its influence.

This attack on Catholicism takes different forms. One is to attempt to discredit the Church in various ways.

Ridicule — of Catholic teachings, institutions, and practices — is a favorite technique of the entertainment media, as well as of radio and television talk-show hosts, political cartoonists, and social activists opposed to the Church's moral teachings.

The objects of such ridicule vary. Sometimes, as with Ted Turner's snide comment to a pro-abortion audience about using Pope John Paul II as "a Polish mine detector," it is Church leaders who are targeted. Other times it is the beliefs, practices, or sacred figures of Catholicism. The April, 1998, final episode of the ABC sitcom *That's Life* managed, in a half-hour's time, to mock virtually every aspect of Catholicism, from

Christ's suffering and death on the Cross, to the sacraments of Penance and the Eucharist, to the faith lives of Catholics and the behavior of priests.

Radio and TV talk-show hosts, as well as political cartoonists, regularly focus on the Church's positions on contemporary issues — not, as a general rule, to afford the Church's views serious treatment, but rather to sarcastically demean and dismiss them.

Whatever the targets, the intent is the same: to make the Catholic Church seem ridiculous so that the public will dismiss its moral teachings out of hand, lest they pose a challenge to the secular values of the cultural elite.

Sometimes this ridicule degenerates further, into blasphemy and defamation. Such was the case with a huge display on the arts page of *Envoy,* the newspaper of Hunter College of the City University of New York, in December, 1998. The display, purporting to advertise "Virgin Mary Immaculate Conception condoms," featured a depiction of Jesus on the Cross, in the throes of crucifixion, wearing a condom on his erect penis. Similarly, the "Condom Communion Mass" sponsored in San Francisco by the "Sisters of Perpetual Indulgence" — a group of gay men who like to dress up as nuns and mock the Church — defamed the most sacred of Catholic sacraments. Other examples abound, particularly in the arts community.

This is hate speech, pure and simple, designed to stir up anti-Catholic passions and to deliberately hurt Catholics by gleefully trampling on that which we Catholics hold sacred.

Another approach to discrediting the Church — and one in which the news media are quite culpable — involves distorting Church history or Church teachings, or giving disproportionate attention to actual or alleged misdeeds by individual Catholics.

Consider, for example, what *Newsweek*'s Kenneth Woodward has aptly termed the "monstrous calumnies" being perpetrated against Pope Pius XII. "Something shameful is going on," Woodward wrote about the concerted effort to portray Pius and the Catholic Church as having been "silent" during the Holocaust — in the face of considerable evidence to the contrary, including expressions of tribute and gratitude from so many leaders of the Jewish community. Yet the news media dutifully report such accusations as accepted truth, without any apparent need to supply evidence, or to even acknowledge the contradictory evidence.

Similarly with the Inquisition, where it is taken as a given that the Catholic Church engaged in years and years of unspeakable cruelties to countless thousands of people. Recent scholarship suggests that the Church in fact exerted a mitigating influence on the harshness of secular authorities. Such research, however, is rarely part of media references to the role of the Catholic Church in the horrors of the Inquisition.

Catholics have also gotten used to seeing disproportionate attention paid to the misdeeds — real or perceived — of individual Catholics. The Center for Media and Public Affairs (CMPA) study notes "the unprecedented level of attention given to charges of criminal behavior by [Catholic] clerics, with particular emphasis on charges of pedophilia and sexual abuse." As *Los Angeles Times* television columnist Howard Rosenberg wrote recently, "Pedophilia (is) an ugly stereotype that's far too broadly applied to priests. Enough already!"

In addition, news reports will often highlight any Catholic connection — no matter how slight or far removed — of someone accused of a particularly heinous crime. We frequently read the terms "former altar boy" or "Catholic school student" attached to a criminal figure in a story — then usually search in vain for references to the religion of any of the other figures in the story who happen not to be Catholic.

Sometimes the accusations turn out not even to be true, but it seems that news media often can't wait to rush the embarrassing story into the headlines. Such was the case with the false allegations of sexual abuse against the late Cardinal Joseph Bernardin, for which CNN later was forced to apologize.

In all of these areas, the strategy is clear — discredit Catholicism by painting Catholics and the Church as hypocrites, whose own sordid misdeeds render them devoid of any moral authority in proclaiming their values to others.

Giving inordinate attention to disagreement with Catholic teachings is yet another means of attempting to discredit the voice of the Church. The CMPA study notes that those news organizations that most frequently cover issues of Catholic doctrine are also most likely to provide forums for dissent from those doctrines. And, while the study notes a decided shift from highlighting internal dissent to focusing on external criticisms, the effect is the same: to call into question the Church's credibility in addressing the issues of the day.

Nowhere is this more evident than in the surge of coverage being given to the question of the role of women in the Church. This issue, the CMPA study found, was "the leading source of controversy" involving news reporting of the Catholic Church in the 1990s, "debated more frequently than all issues involving Church-state relations and Church teachings on sexual morality combined."

Moreover, this "concentration" on women's issues "was nearly matched by the consensus of views expressed on these issues" — a consensus overwhelmingly negative. "Three out of four sources criticized the Church's treatment of women," the study notes, with "over 90 per cent of sources on TV news" being "critical of the Church." Indeed, the entity which "came closest to balanced coverage" on this issue was *The New York*

Times, where opinions were still weighted against the Church by 61 to 39 percent.

That the role of women was the predominant issue in a shift of attention from doctrinal issues to "power relations within the Church" reflects an effort to discredit the Church's message by discrediting Church leaders. When we see that women's issues and issues of sexual morality account for two thirds of the news coverage of controversies within the Church, the message comes into focus: Given that issues like abortion, divorce, and birth control are commonly characterized as "women's issues," the "male-dominated, patriarchal" Catholic Church is in no position to offer moral guidance on these issues. Thus does this new focus on women's issues in the Church apply the tried and true pro-abortion strategy: Avoid at all costs directly debating the merits of a moral issue, and instead appeal to anti-Catholic bigotry to discredit the Catholic position.

Besides such varied attempts to discredit the Church, the cultural elite also seek to exploit the teachings, practices, and imagery of Catholicism to promote agendas that are antithetical to Catholic values.

Terrence McNally's ill-fated play, *Corpus Christi,* was an example. By portraying Jesus as a promiscuous homosexual, McNally was using the revered figure of Christ as a vehicle for promoting acceptance of the gay lifestyle; at the same time he was distorting Christ's message of love and forgiveness to condemn those who uphold traditional Judeo-Christian teachings against homosexual activity.

It has become almost routine for those promoting the use of condoms to do so by exploiting and defaming Catholic beliefs. Take, for example, Levi Strauss's 1998 "Condom Christmas Tree" gambit. In December, 1998, Levi Strauss made plans to erect a Christmas tree at the Wollman skating rink in Central

Park and decorate it with thousands of brightly colored condoms. Strauss was denied permission to desecrate Christmas in this manner only after a strong protest launched by the Catholic League.

Similarly, Planned Parenthood of Connecticut used the celebration of St. Patrick's Day to distribute green condoms in the state capitol, with such slogans on them as "Kiss me, I'm Irish," "Put on the Green," and "Four Leaf Cover." And, of course, the "Holy Communion Condom" distributed by the "Sisters of Perpetual Indulgence" in San Francisco was just one of many examples of this group's effort to exploit and demean the Church for its own ends. Another such example (see Chapter 1, page 52) was the group's use of Easter Sunday — with the blessing of the city government of San Francisco — to celebrate the anniversary of its founding with more ridicule of the Catholic Church.

The strategy here is to once again belittle and discredit traditional Catholic beliefs and to suggest that the reason Catholicism is so ridiculous is that it so distorts what Jesus really taught — which, of course, is far closer to their agenda than to Catholic tradition. Faithful Catholics hear Jesus' message of personal restraint and responsibility. The cultural elite transform Christ into a sexual hedonist who embraces their lifestyle, and whose true teachings would endorse their promotion of condoms and other panaceas to avoid personal responsibility for the consequences of that lifestyle.

While some thus exploit anti-Catholicism to promote a larger agenda, others engage in such exploitation for pure — and shameless — self-promotion. Throughout the spring and summer of 1998, an "artist" in Seattle displayed increasingly vile, blasphemous, anti-Catholic paintings in a back-street, hole-in-the-wall art gallery known as Art/Not Terminal. The artist and his supporters continually e-mailed the Catholic League, trying to provoke a controversy that would gain him some desperately needed notoriety. The league learned that the artist was also contacting local media in Seattle, trying to get them to stir up such a controversy. When that failed to gain him the attention he wanted, he took to defaming league president William Donohue in his paintings and adding the Catholic League logo to his displays.

A similar incident in New York City in early 1999 had an artist's agent contacting the league about his client's version of the Pietà — depicting Mary in bondage. In Albany in March, 1999, a producer lamented that his staging of *The Pope and the Witch,* an anti-Catholic play by Dario Fo, had not generated more controversy.

Such incidents are significant for what they say about perceptions of anti-Catholicism in modern American society: that it is so prevalent and so acceptable that it can be exploited to the *advantage* of artists willing to engage in Catholic-bashing.

How the media handle such efforts to exploit anti-Catholicism is crucial to their chances for success. To its credit, the Seattle media largely ignored the Art/Not Terminal displays. *New York* magazine, on the other hand, peppered the Catholic League with calls about the "bondage" Pietà, apparently after having been prompted by the same agent who contacted the league. And the *Albany Times Union* gave the producer of *The Pope and the Witch* a forum to promote the film's anti-Catholic nature.

Another manifestation of anti-Catholicism designed to negate the Church's voice involves a blatant assault on the rights of Catholics, both to practice their religion and to be heard on the great moral and social issues of the day.

In San Diego, on Ash Wednesday, 1997, a woman went to work at the Silvergate Retirement Residence with ashes on her forehead, only to be ordered by her supervisor to remove them. When she refused, the supervisor took a rag and wiped the ashes from her forehead. Only after the Catholic League intervened was the supervisor disciplined and the woman apologized to.

Another victim denied his right to publicly express his Catholic faith was Zachary Hood, a six-year-old boy from Medford, New Jersey. When Zachary's first-grade teacher instructed all her students to bring one of their favorite stories to read to the class, Zachary selected an Old Testament story from his children's Bible. President Clinton's 1995 directives on religion in the schools state unequivocally that "students may express their beliefs about religion in the form of homework, artwork, and other written and oral assignments free of discrimination based on the religious content of their submissions." Nevertheless, the teacher refused to let Zachary read his story in class, sending the six-year-old boy home in tears.

On a broader scale Catholic schools, while denied government funds under the guise of "separation of Church and State," have found themselves subject to governmental intrusion. Last spring, St. John's Literary Institute in Maryland endeavored to expel two students for engaging in inappropriate sexual contact in a school hallway. The parents sued and succeeded in obtaining an injunction blocking the school from expelling the students. In that case, a higher court reversed the ruling and upheld the right of this Catholic school to implement its own disciplinary procedures free from government interference.

In November, 1998, however, Archbishop Shaw High School in Louisiana faced a similar situation, when it suspended two student football stars who had been arrested on charges of the attempted rape of a fifteen-year-old girl. A judge blocked the suspension, forcing the school not only to allow the two boys to remain in the school but also to continue playing on the football team. The boys subsequently transferred out of the school voluntarily, rendering the case moot, but leaving unchallenged this instance of government encroachment into the autonomy of Catholic schools.

Stifling of the Catholic voice in public debate is another facet of this frontal assault on the rights of Catholics. This, too, takes several forms — one of the most prevalent being a double standard when it comes to religious involvement in politics.

The New York Times provided a textbook example just before Election Day, 1998. A page one roundup story on significant campaign activities noted — without comment — that Rep. Charles Schumer, campaigning for the U.S. Senate, had given a campaign speech in a Protestant church, and that President Clinton, joined by several statewide candidates, had delivered a highly partisan campaign speech during Sunday service at a Protestant church in Maryland.

A second *Times* article, on the same day, focused on the role of "Churches" in the political campaign. The only church mentioned, however, was New York's St. Patrick's Cathedral, where Cardinal John O'Connor deplored efforts to link himself — and, by extension, pro-life political candidates — to the shooting of an abortionist some weeks earlier. The *Times* reporter sought out Planned Parenthood director Alexander Sanger, who dutifully accused the cardinal of "making a political statement."

There was no mention in this article of the appearance of Rep. Schumer at a Protestant service, or of the Protestant church in Maryland turning its Sunday service into a pre-election partisan political rally. Cardinal O'Connor, however — who mentioned no candidates' names and afforded none the use of his pulpit — is accused of meddling in politics because he preached about a moral issue.

Similarly, when the U.S. bishops, in *Living the Gospel of Life,* exhorted Catholic public officials "to place their faith at the heart of their public service" by defending life, there was an outpouring of media commentary warning that the bishops were treading over the "wall of separation between Church and State," and in the process jeopardizing their tax-exempt status and inviting anti-Catholic reaction.

Catholic Church involvement in Oregon's debate on assisted suicide in 1997 was met with a steady barrage of anti-Catholic hostility. A radio talk-show host repeatedly asserted that the Church's participation in the debate represented a "foreign government" interfering in Oregon politics, and the state's chief petitioner in favor of assisted suicide, Barbara Coombs Lee, declared that the state legislature had been "taken hostage" by "the raw political power of the Catholic Church."

The approach here is not just to disagree with the Church's position on a public policy issue, but to question the Church's right to speak at all. The *Northeast Times* in Philadelphia, for example, responded to Cardinal Anthony Bevilacqua's public opposition to same-sex "life partnerships" legislation by scolding him for entering "the public pulpit" instead of restricting himself to "those on the altars of churches."

Another technique in stifling the Catholic voice is to attack those Catholics in public life who *do* place their faith at the heart of their public service.

In Wisconsin, for example, after the State Supreme Court upheld the inclusion of religious schools in Milwaukee's educational voucher program, Ann Nicol Gaylor of the Freedom From Religion Foundation found it "ominous" that the majority of judges on the court were Catholic. She also railed against "Wisconsin's Catholic governor, Tommy Thompson," for having "appointed so many Catholics to positions of power that the statehouse resembles a Catholic club."

During the Congressional impeachment of President Clinton, House Judiciary Committee Chairman Rep. Henry Hyde and chief counsel for the Judiciary Committee David Schippers found their Catholicism attacked by media supporters of the president. Hyde was accused of targeting Clinton because of the president's strong pro-abortion policies, and Cheryl McCarthy of *Newsday* mocked Hyde's Catholic faith while portraying the impeachment trial as an Inquisition. Judy Mann of *The Washington Post,* criticizing Schippers's arguments for impeachment, suddenly found herself off on a tangent mocking the teachings of his Catholic faith on heaven and hell.

Efforts to exclude the Catholic perspective from the public debate extend beyond political issues, even striking at the Church's social services network.

Hospital mergers involving Catholic health care facilities have become a favorite target of late. Story after story, in print and broadcast media, as well as numerous opinion pieces, warn of the dearth of "reproductive services" (that is, abortion, contraception, sterilization, in vitro fertilization) that will result from community hospitals accepting Catholic moral and ethical standards in order to merge with Catholic facilities.

Virtually nowhere do we read or hear of the many services that will be preserved, because the infusion of resources from Catholic health care facilities will make it possible for many of these community hospitals to remain open. Nor do we read or hear about "freedom of choice" — which was supposed to be the centerpiece of the Supreme Court's *Roe* and *Griswold* decisions legalizing abortion and contraception — as it applies to the right of private hospitals to choose not to provide these "services." Instead, the Catholic health care network is portrayed as a threat to women's health, and the Church-State double standard arises again, as with Jennifer Baumgardner's article in *Nation* magazine (January 25, 1999) calling for the use of anti-discrimination laws to force Catholic hospitals to perform abortions.

The teachings of the Catholic Church are challenging. Based on an understanding of the transcendent meaning of human life, they challenge us to adhere to fundamental standards of right and wrong grounded in natural law. They challenge us to live lives of service to God and to our fellow human beings. They challenge us to practice humility and self-denial, understanding that all that we are comes from God.

The Church teaches that it is in meeting those challenges, and in understanding and accepting the transcendent meaning of our lives, that we have the opportunity to achieve true happiness.

While not all will agree, a truly pluralistic society would welcome the Catholic perspective. Indeed, the success of a democratic society depends on such free exchange of ideas and respectful give-and-take between competing points of view.

To America's cultural elite, however, the Catholic perspective is deserving of no respect. To them the Church's teachings pose not a challenge, but a threat. Talk of self-denial, of personal responsibility, or of a transcendent standard of right and wrong strikes fear in their hearts, because it challenges a lifestyle dominated by the constant pursuit of personal pleasure.

Such thinking cannot be met simply with respectful disagreement. To do so would confer a respectability on the Catholic perspective that might allow it to actually impact the culture — to the detriment of the transient values of the secular age.

Instead, the Catholic Church must be discredited, its teachings distorted and ridiculed, its voice stifled in the public square. It is fear of Catholicism — and of the challenges our Catholic faith presents — that drives the anti-Catholicism of America's cultural elite.

Rick Hinshaw is associate director of communications for the New York State Catholic Conference and is the former director of communications for the Catholic League for Religious and Civil Rights. Hinshaw has an M.A. in political science from C. W. Post Center of Long Island University.

CHAPTER ✦ 4

The Church and the Media: Who's to Blame?

By Russell Shaw

In case there was ever any doubt about it, *Media Coverage of the Catholic Church 1963-1998* makes it clear that during the 1990s two big Catholic stories got special notice from national news media: clergy sex abuse and the controversy over women's issues. This was not good news for the Church. Several things should be said about it at the start.

The first thing is that, by any definition of news, these really were important stories. The media did not invent them, nor is it clear that they greatly overplayed them. Whether the stories were covered fairly in all respects is another matter — and I shall explain later why I think they weren't. Still, the mere fact that these stories were a conspicuous part of the coverage of the Church during 1990s does not by itself demonstrate media bias.

Second, to some extent both of these stories display the Church shooting itself in the foot, albeit in somewhat different ways. This is true of their substance and also of the way they were handled. Clergy sex scandals and women's issues are instances where Church people, including some in positions of authority, brought much of the grief, though not all of it, on themselves — and on the rest of us, too. I shall say more about that also.

The third point may also be the most controversial. The media environment wherein sexual abuse by priests and the Church's approach to women became big stories is in fundamental conflict with Catholic beliefs and practices. As a result, the coverage was worse for the Church than would otherwise have been the case. For the most part, the problem is neither personal hostility on the part of journalists nor the self-consciously anti-Catholic bigotry of earlier times. It is impersonal and ideological — the instinctive dislike that postmodern secularism harbors toward a world view correctly perceived as an obstacle to some of its most cherished goals.

The executive summary of *Media Coverage of the Catholic Church 1963-1998* says in part:

> As it has over the past four decades, the coverage again emphasized the need for the Church to adapt to the more egalitarian and democratic norms and procedures that characterize the secular institutions of American society. In the 1990s this perspective focused mainly on the Church's treatment of women and heightened attention to clerical wrongdoing. As we found in our earlier study, this was not a matter of overtly opinionated or muckraking coverage. It would be more accurate to see it as the reflection of the prism through which one institution — the media — views another with very different norms and traditions.

Given that underlying reality, the Church's mistakes in confronting two crises of such magnitude and sensitivity as women's issues and clergy sex abuse look well-nigh suicidal.

In order to make sense of the analysis that follows, it will be necessary to sketch the cultural situation of the Catholic Church in the United States and the media environment in which the Church has to protect its interests and pursue its mission. Having done that, I shall take a closer look at these two big Catholic stories of the 1990s. Finally, I shall draw some practical conclusions.

The Cultural Situation of the Catholic Church in the U.S.

How do the Catholic Church and American secular culture relate to each other? How should they relate? Catholics and non-Catholics have discussed these questions since colonial times. People with an animus against the Church have tended to think of it as an alien presence in conflict with American values. For their part, some Catholics have come close to equating Catholicism and the American way. Today, most people probably stand somewhere in the middle: The Catholic Church has a legitimate place in America, but mainly on the culture's terms.

Assimilation always has been a central issue for Catholics. In his shrewdly written popular history, *American Catholic: The Saints and Sinners Who Built America's Most Powerful Church* (Times Books, 1997), Charles R. Morris frames it like this: "Can the Church assimilate and survive? Or must it assimilate *to* survive?" There are two very different views on that.

They can be seen at work in the case of two prominent Catholic converts of the nineteenth century, the social thinker and writer Orestes Brownson (1803-1876) and the founder of the Paulists, Father Isaac Hecker (1819-1888). At one time these two friends took much the same view of the relationship between religion and politics in America, deeming it fundamentally friendly and beneficial to both; but Brownson eventually grew disillusioned, even as Hecker continued to regard American democracy as a congenial setting for religion.

A defining moment occurred in January, 1899, when Pope Leo XIII published an apostolic letter, *Testem Benevolentiae*, condemning something called Americanism. He took exception to a number of ideas attributed to this source: that, for the sake of evangelization, the Church should "come closer to the civilization of this advanced age, and relaxing its old severity show indulgence to those opinions and theories of the people which have recently been introduced"; or, again, that "in order to win over those who are in disagreement," it is desirable that "certain topics of doctrine [be] passed over as of lesser importance, or [be] so softened that they do not retain the same sense as the Church has always held." Novel thinking about the virtues and about religious life giving preference to activism over contemplation also was examined and rejected.

Did anybody really hold such views? The ideas condemned by Leo XIII seem to have had more of a home in France than in the United States. Although there is a family resemblance between some of them and certain of Hecker's ideas, it might well be an exaggeration to attribute any of these views literally to him. Leading figures in the Americanist wing of U.S. Catholicism were quick to deny that such notions had any currency here.

Although *Testem Benevolentiae* sent a chill through certain ecclesiastical circles in the United States, the main thrust of the Americanist movement was not thereby deflected. In fact, it seems fair to say that in the century since then, Americanist thinking in a general sense, if not precisely the sense spelled out by Leo XIII, became conventional wisdom for what is often called "the American Church."

More than just good-hearted love of country, the essence of it is an uncritical version of enculturation that takes it for granted that assimilation into American culture is easily compatible with being Catholic. This is an option for institutions as much as for individuals. Archbishop John Ireland of St. Paul, the most prominent Americanist of his day, caught the spirit of it in an address to a French audience in 1892:

> In America we have a free Church in a free country, and the church is happy in her freedom. . . . The fu-

ture of the Catholic Church in America is bright and encouraging. To people in other countries, American Catholicism presents features which seem unusual; these features are the result of the freedom which our civil and political institutions give us. . . . By word and act we prove that we are patriots of patriots. Our hearts always beat with love for the republic. Our tongues are always eloquent in celebrating her praises. Our hands are always uplifted to bless her banners and her soldiers.

This jingoistic rhetoric expresses a deep and abiding desire for acceptance by America, together with the deep-seated conviction that there is no conflict — indeed, there is easy interaction and mutual support — between Catholicism and the surrounding culture. Whatever popes or anyone else might have to say about "Americanism," such sentiments were taken for granted by most American Catholics throughout the twentieth century.

Naïve Americanism helped to pave the way for the cultural assimilation of Catholics that began to occur at an accelerating pace in the century's middle years. So, on a very different intellectual plane, did the efforts of Father John Courtney Murray, S.J., who in the 1950s polished central principles of the Americanist creed to a sophisticated high gloss. In his influential book *We Hold These Truths* (Sheed and Ward, 1960), the Jesuit theologian argued not just that the Catholic Church was entitled to feel at home in America, but that the natural law tradition nurtured by the Church was the basis of the American system.

Dying in 1967, Murray lived long enough to see the early, breakthrough victories of the cultural revolution of that era but not the revolution's triumph in the bourgeois libertarian ethic of choice that came to dominate American secular culture by century's end. To his credit, he foresaw the dire consequences of abandoning the social consensus grounded in natural law in favor of positivism and moral relativism. The result would be a disastrous depleting of what now is fashionably termed "social capital" in academic circles that, by jettisoning natural law, did so much to bring about the dispersal of social capital they bemoan.

Were something like that to happen, Murray wrote, then the idea would take hold that "all human values . . . are manmade, and in consequence all human 'rights' . . . look only to man for their creation, realization, and guarantee." Then law would be seen as "a pure instrumentality whereby lawmakers and judges, recognizing the human desires that are seeking realization at a given moment in human society, endeavor to satisfy these desires with a minimum of social friction." That is just what has happened in the case of abortion (although, as critics like Justice Ruth Bader Ginsburg point out, the Supreme Court blundered by not anticipating the "social friction" that would result from its abortion decisions of 1973 and heading it off by a gradualist approach to legalization); now it is threatening again in the cases of assisted suicide and euthanasia, homosexual marriage, and other practices approved by the secular elite.

To the extent that they are assimilated into this American culture, Catholics have no great difficulty accepting such things. Many studies of the beliefs and attitudes of assimilated Catholics show them mirroring the culture more closely than they reflect the Catholic tradition. The data also show that Catholics (and Protestants) who regularly attend church are far more likely to adhere to traditional standards of belief and behavior than those who do not; but even among regular churchgoers, the inroads of assimilation, reinforced by theological dissent and a pervasive failure of catechesis, are visible.

Something else also has been happening since the middle years of the century to speed assimilation. As Charles Morris points out, by the 1940s and 1950s the great strength of American Catholicism lay in the existence of a thriving Catholic subculture, painstakingly built up over the previous century and sustained by a vast network of programs, organizations, and institutions that supported Catholics in their religious identity and, as time went by, increasingly empowered them to address American secular culture on equal terms and shape it in light of Catholic values. One need not romanticize this American Catholic subculture or ignore its many faults — narrowness and parochialism, clericalism and triumphalism, superficiality and lack of intellectual and spiritual depth — in order to see that, taken as a whole and in the context of its times, it was a huge success.

And, to a considerable extent, Catholics themselves dismantled it and threw it away. Perhaps something like that would have happened anyway — although it is at least possible that the subculture and its institutions could have been updated and adapted to changing times. Instead the process was consciously hastened by the deliberate choices and acts of members of Catholic elite groups (academics, some members of the clergy, writers and journalists), convinced that the Church in America, having come of age, no longer needed this puerile, sectarian system of supports. Those were giddy days. Beginning in the late 1950s with a concerted critique of Catholic higher education, Morris says, American Catholic intellectuals "embarked on a fearsome exercise. It was nothing less than the dangerous and potentially catastrophic project of severing the connection between the Catholic religion and the . . . American Catholic culture that had always been the source of its dynamism, its appeal, and its power."

By now that project has largely succeeded. The Catholic

subculture of the past is no more. What has taken its place is only the shadow of what was. As a result, American Catholics often seem defenseless against the forces of assimilation, alternately seductive and coercive, marshaled against them by secular culture.

The Media Environment

Media make up a great part of the cultural context for American Catholics today. This environment has been described in many places, including the first Lichter report, *Media Coverage of the Catholic Church*, published in 1991, and now Lichter-II, *Media Coverage of the Catholic Church 1963-1998*. Rather than repeat what is said in these studies (see Part II of this book), I shall suggest the nature of the media environment with an anecdote.

One day in early December of 1992, I found myself at the campuslike headquarters of the Educational Testing Service in Princeton, New Jersey. ETS is an important research center and think tank, as well as a giant in the field of standardized testing, and I had been invited by a senior researcher, a friend from high-school days, who had directed a project resulting in a newly published book. (It is called *Sources of Inspiration* and was published by Sheed and Ward in 1992.) Secular journalists profiled fifteen religious figures representing — in the words of the foreword — "exemplary pastoral practice." A couple of dozen people had been assembled this day — some of those profiled in the book, some of the journalists (including present and former staff members of *The New York Times, The Washington Post, The Los Angeles Times,* and other major news organizations), staff members from ETS and other think tanks, two representatives of the Catholic press, and me. The assignment was to dialogue about the media and religion.

As the hours wore on, I became uneasy at first, then annoyed. The church people were deferential to the press, while the journalists, adopting a patronizing tone, insisted that the media wanted nothing so much as to give religion a hand. This did not much resemble religion-media relations as I had experienced them.

In saying they wanted to help religion, it became clear the journalists meant the kind of religion represented in the book — religion that suited secular tastes. Clearly, they did *not* mean the Mormons or the Christian Coalition or Islamic fundamentalists or the tiny Bruderhof communities or any other groups cut off from the mainstream of secular acceptability. Nor did they mean the version of Roman Catholicism I happened to favor — a version that assigns an active, constructive social role to religion but also places a premium on orthodox doctrine.

In midafternoon I finally took the floor and said my piece.

"From a historical perspective," I began, "anti-Catholicism has been a problem in the United States for a long time. There even is a history of anti-Catholicism in American journalism."

I had gotten my audience's attention.

"Still," I went on, "I don't think old-fashioned anti-Catholicism today is the problem that it once was — I mean the kind of anti-Catholicism that's hostile in principle to all things Catholic. It still exists of course, but it isn't socially acceptable any more.

"The more serious problem now is a new kind of anti-Catholicism. Perhaps anti-Catholicism isn't even the right word for it, and I am careful these days not to speak casually about 'anti-Catholicism' without using qualifiers. But whatever it should be called, this new thing is very visible in the media.

"It amounts to taking sides in the intramural quarrels of Catholics. Naturally, the media tend to favor the liberal side.

To illustrate that, I call your attention to the op-ed page of *The New York Times* and the Anna Quindlen column."

Anna Quindlen since then has quit daily journalism to write fiction, but at that time she was a widely read *Times* columnist, a winner of the Pulitzer Prize. She also was, and I assume still is, a Catholic, a feminist, and an ardent supporter of legalized abortion. Rather often she used her column to declare her views on all three subjects — Catholicism, feminism, and abortion — while excoriating Pope John Paul II and Cardinal John O'Connor of New York.

"Anna Quindlen is a very talented journalist," I continued. "The *Times* is fortunate to have her and is certainly entitled to publish her. I don't question that at all.

"But, just to illustrate the problem I speak of, let me ask this: Would *The New York Times* regularly give Cardinal O'Connor the same space to air his views on Catholic doctrine regarding sex and abortion that it gives to Anna Quindlen? Or, if that's unrealistic — and I'm sure it is — would the *Times* give the same opportunity to someone else who thinks pretty much the way the cardinal and Pope John Paul do? The answer is obvious, of course — and that's the problem in a nutshell."

My remarks were not well received.

A former education writer for *The New York Times,* now with Educational Testing Service, asked huffily if I thought the paper should not carry the Quindlen column. Since I had specifically said it was entitled to do that, the question did not strike me as helpful. That's not the point, I said.

Well then, he demanded, what *did* I think the *Times* ought to do?

Not for me to say, I replied. I'm just trying to describe a problem, not tell the editors of *The New York Times* how to edit their paper.

But it was left to another former *Times* writer to make the most telling rejoinder. This was an African American woman who recently had left the paper to do freelance writing. Earlier in the day she had made it a point to tell us all that she had been raised Catholic but had quit the Church because it oppressed women and blacks.

Anna Quindlen gets a lot of hate mail, she began. ("There are crazies everywhere," I replied. I might have added that I get hate mail, too — it is an occupational hazard for anyone who puts ideas in print.) But the heart of her message was a blunt defense of just the kind of ideological tilt I had spoken about. This is how she put it:

"Our secular society has certain needs and imperatives of its own. And it will satisfy those needs and it will act on those imperatives, no matter who objects. And if you and people like you don't like it . . . that's *your* problem!"

Exactly. I could not have said it better myself. Our elite media are an integral part of the secular culture. Journalists not only transmit that culture's values but also serve as its enforcers, rewarding people who conform and punishing those who do not. How do they reward and punish? Mainly, with "good coverage" and "bad coverage," praise and blame. And, of course, sometimes with no coverage at all: the cultural death of being ignored. All this adds up to a highly effective mechanism for encouraging cultural assimilation and conformity.

Lichter-I, the first version of *Media Coverage of the Catholic Church*, pointed to this conclusion, among others. In the introduction to a volume containing proceedings of a conference held to discuss that study (*Anti-Catholicism in the Media,* Our Sunday Visitor, 1993), Patrick Riley and I spelled it out:

> There is . . . ample evidence here that Catholic dissent received copious and respectful attention from these

media over the past three decades, while the beliefs and values of Catholics loyal to the magisterium of their Church did not fare so well. . . . The mind-set in elite American media — call it secularism, call it the liberal zeitgeist, call it postmodern deconstructionist individualism — has found a better way to undermine the Catholic Church than was ever dreamed of by the old, religiously-inspired anti-Catholicism. It has learned to be selective and reward dissent.

Lichter-II makes it clear that this problem did not disappear in the 1990s.

My experience at ETS was unusual, but only because the truth of these matters does not very often get spoken, especially by journalists strongly attached to the myth of their objectivity and ideological disinterestedness. Journalists usually try commendably hard to be honest, but on this subject they are as likely as anybody else to practice self-deception. Still, truth-telling occasionally does happen.

The volume of proceedings just mentioned contains a highly illuminating paper by Richard Harwood, a veteran newsman who then was ombudsman of *The Washington Post* and later wrote a *Post* column dealing mainly with the news business. His remarks about the relationship between the media and religion were a lot more candid and informed than what gets said about this topic by either church people or journalists usually is.

Remarking laconically that the "secular character of our newspapers is not totally divorced from the interests or character of the people who produce them," Harwood noted the finding — in studies by Robert Lichter and others — that journalists with elite news organizations commonly have "weak" religious attachments. "That is true in my own case and is consistent with my impression of my colleagues," he said. "We were educated in secular institutions, are quite sensitive to changing fashions in secular intellectual thought and to the pseudo-secularism preached in many pulpits."

Still, he pointed out, the analysis cannot end with the media but must extend to the Church. As far as the Catholic Church was concerned, the "great intersection" of its doctrinal views with "the political affairs of this secular society" had become newsworthy. And, as a result of the "intrusion of religious bodies and individuals into secular affairs," religion in general and the Catholic Church in particular had suffered "demystification, a loss of deference, and an erosion of institutional standing."

In other words, the Church is welcome to think whatever it pleases about things like abortion and assisted suicide, and even to try to persuade its adherents to think the same; but secular journalists will not pay attention to its views until it attempts to apply them to the political order — a form of activity Harwood significantly termed "intrusion." When that happens, the Church's values and beliefs do become news; but it forfeits whatever privileges or exemptions from rough handling it might previously have enjoyed in the days when it was being ignored.

Of course this applies to other churches and religious groups besides the Catholic Church. It appears to me — and the Lichter studies tend to support this — that the Church took its worst pounding from the media over politics in the 1970s, when it was very nearly the only national voice opposing the policy of legalized abortion then newly mandated by the Supreme Court. More recently, it has been the turn of politically active evangelical Protestants. In a notorious incident in 1993, a *Washington Post* writer casually described the viewers of television evangelists as "largely poor, uneducated and easy to command"; flooded with protests, the newspaper conceded that there was no factual basis for saying that.

Richard Harwood next addressed the finding that, in news coverage of controversies about Church teaching, sources critical of the teaching outnumbered sources supporting it:

> One reason for the disparity of numbers is . . . that the position of the Church on many of these issues is a minority position among Americans in general and quite possibly among American Catholics as well. I think people who ignore the teachings on birth control probably far exceed those who observe them.
>
> The teachings on contraception, in my view, really have no intellectual standing in our society outside the Church, and perhaps with a minority within the Church. Possibly that could be said of other issues. But as journalists we are under no obligation to give superior weight or credence to an institutional declaration of the Pope or the cardinals or whatever. . . .
>
> The story of religion in America is starting to resemble other stories. It has come to resemble a great political story. It has begun to have high-profile scandals, and all the rest. It is becoming less of an institutional story which can be handled by covering established bodies and their actions. Religion . . . is becoming more diverse and privatized, and is finding its way into the news in new and different ways and places.
>
> I think that is what we are seeing today in our newspapers and in the other media. There is no question whatever that these media are secular institutions. There is no question that secular thought is the preferred body of thought within the media. . . . We should not be surprised at that because these media mirror the popular culture. I

think that is not going to change; and if Bob Lichter comes back a few years from now and does a similar study, he is going to get the same results.

It is in this media environment, as described by Richard Harwood, that the Catholic Church in the United States now exists.

The Catholic Stories of the 1990s

Midway through a largely positive treatment of contemporary Catholic seminarians, published in *The New York Times* magazine on Easter Sunday, 1999, one abruptly comes across the following:

> The conversation drifts to another, darker presumption about the sexuality of priests. Magat recalls an encounter he had recently in a supermarket. "I was standing in line in my clerics," he says. "The woman in front of me was checking out her groceries, and her young son in the shopping cart, probably 2 or 3, he was kind of looking at me, interested. I waved and said, 'Hi, how's it going?' and she pulled him out of the cart and away from me. I was just mortified."

The writer, Jennifer Egan, adds: "Despite the high profile of the scandals involving the sexual abuse of minors by Catholic priests, there is no evidence that the incidence of sexual misconduct is greater among priests than among clergy of other denominations or the population at large." But, as the anecdote suggests, the damage has been done: In recent years, not a few people have come to look upon Catholic priests as likely child molesters. A reading of *Media Coverage of the Catholic Church 1963-1998* points to the conclusion that the way the media handled this story has a lot to do with that.

In saying this, I do not mean to minimize the problem itself. For clergy to engage in pedophilia is a gross betrayal of trust. It is profoundly shocking that several hundred Catholic priests in the United States (as well as an unknown number in other countries) apparently were guilty of this offense in the last three decades. Nor, it seems, did the ecclesiastical authorities greatly distinguish themselves in this crisis. In the past, when a case like this came to the attention of a bishop or religious superior, the common response seems to have been to scold the offender, possibly ship him off for a brief spell of therapy in a residential setting, then give him another assignment. Although that mirrored the conventional wisdom of the time (as late as the mid-1970s, standard psychiatric texts either said little about pedophiles or tended to make light of the condition), this does not explain, much less justify, the continued resort to inadequate measures in the case of repeat offenders.

The problem first became widely known in 1984 when a priest in Lafayette, Louisiana, went on trial on charges of sexual molestation. (For this and many other details I am indebted to *Pedophiles and Priests: Anatomy of a Contemporary Crisis,* published by Oxford University Press in 1996. The book is the work of Philip Jenkins, a professor of history and religious studies at Pennsylvania State University who has written several studies of the way issues become distorted in the media and in public opinion.) Disclosures of other cases in other parts of the country quickly followed. By August, 1990, more than a thousand cases of sex abuse by clergy, non-Catholic as well as Catholic, were reported to be in the courts. By 1994, some sixty priests had been jailed.

The public response on the part of Church authorities was

inept in the early years. The media relations strategy of diocesan officials, presumably acting on lawyers' advice, was to decline comment. Perhaps this was smart from a legal point of view. But where the Church's reputation and credibility are at stake, silence often is exactly the wrong approach, for it suggests guilty knowledge, indifference to accountability, and a commitment to institutional considerations above everything else.

From a time early in the crisis, it is now clear, considerable information was available to the National Conference of Catholic Bishops. I was aware that on one or two occasions the bishops had discussed the problem, and even heard presentations by lawyers and mental health professionals, during executive sessions of their general meeting. But neither I nor any other communication official of the national organization was privy to what was going on, nor were we consulted about the media aspects of the situation. I have to admit, though, that this suited me well enough, since, like a lot of other people, I found the whole subject distasteful and was glad I could truthfully tell reporters I knew almost nothing about it. Like many others in those early years, too, I assumed that there were only a handful of isolated cases, and once these were disposed of, the crisis would pass.

Since then, the bishops' conference has adopted a more sensible approach. The problem has been discussed publicly at bishops' general meetings. A committee of bishops has been established to monitor the matter and make recommendations and periodic reports. Moreover, as Lichter-II points out, the dignity and forbearance with which the late Cardinal Joseph Bernardin handled false accusations of sexual abuse earned public sympathy.

Unfortunately, these changes occurred after the worst harm was done. What Jenkins calls a "sinister and unsavory vision of the Church" gained currency, spreading especially into movies and TV entertainment programming. Almost certainly some new vocations to the priesthood were discouraged; the morale of good priests was hurt; and the respect of the Catholic people for their clergy was eroded.

Yet pedophilia is certainly not confined to the clergy, nor is it any more of a problem among Catholic priests than clergy of other denominations. A few years ago it was estimated that about two percent of American priests — one thousand out of fifty thousand — were, or had been, involved with minors. Most were not true pedophiles but had homosexual relationships with older youths; the abusers of children apparently numbered in the hundreds.

But the media gave the impression that pedophilia *was* a Catholic priest problem — indeed, that the problem was endemic to priests. Moreover, as Jenkins points out, "both print and visual media offered remarkably condemnatory interpretations of church actions, and found themselves in alliance with the reform agendas of dissident Catholic groups. Consciously or otherwise, the secular media were claiming a role in the making of internal church policies."

Lustful priests and hypocritical bishops are stock figures in anti-Catholic literature of the 1800s and early 1900s, and in this new situation the media drew to some extent on those hostile stereotypes. But the coverage of the pedophilia story also reflected a secular judgment on Catholic sexual mores that has become widespread since the 1960s: This is the self-serving judgment of a sexually libertarian culture that the Church's ascetical ideal — including priestly celibacy — is psychologically harmful and a cause of aberrant behavior.

As on many other occasions over the years, the media looked to representatives of the Catholic left for guidance in interpreting this controversy. The story broke nationally in the pages of the *National Catholic Reporter,* which then proceeded to serve up explanations of the abuse problem that, Jenkins says, would have caused the secular media to be branded "overtly anti-Catholic" if the same explanations had originated there. In time, too, a group of self-selected "experts" on clergy sex abuse — almost invariably, "progressive" Catholics — began turning up regularly in the media. Church authorities were treated only as foils and targets. Traditional Catholics were, as usual, ignored by journalists as if they did not exist.

The crimes of clerical pedophiles deserved to be exposed. In fact, if the actions of some had been brought to light in their dioceses in the 1960s and 1970s, there might have been a lot fewer cases waiting to be disclosed, with such devastating results, in the 1980s and 1990s. But that does not cancel out the fact that the media coverage of this crisis became increasingly sensationalized as time went by. And in this way the harm was compounded.

The second big Catholic story of the 1990s, as reported by *Media Coverage of the Catholic Church,* concerned women's issues. Lichter-II correctly puts it under the heading "Power Relations in the Church," since, as the argument is shaped by the interaction of feminism and clericalism, it really is a dispute about power. The results, in media terms, are reflected in this from *Media Coverage:*

> The concentration of debate on "women's issues" was nearly matched by the consensus of views expressed on these issues. Three out of four opinions on the role of women in the Church (75 percent) urged change or reform; only one out of four (25 percent) supported current practices. . . . During the current decade, debate coalesced around the role of women. This included both questions of ordination and the general status of women

in the church. The new prominence of women's rights issues was especially important to overall perceptions of the Church, because this proved to be an area in which the media debate was sharply tilted in favor of change.

Note that "current practices" in this context include the exclusion of women from ordination as priests. (Similarly, anyone trying to follow this debate within the Church should understand that generalities like "more authority for women" and "a larger role for women" are code terms that commonly include priestly ordination — along with other things, of course.)

While the coverage of women's issues is different from the coverage of clerical sex abuse in important ways, there also are important likenesses. In both cases there was, and perhaps to some extent still is, a serious substantive problem; in both, policy mistakes have made matters worse; and, in both, coverage by the secular media tilted against traditional Catholic beliefs and practices.

Historically, the Catholic Church has been a force for women's dignity and rights, but in modern times it hardly has been at the cutting edge. During the 1971 world Synod of Bishops in Rome, one of the American delegates asked me to draft an intervention on the subject of women. Lacking any original ideas, I produced a short text saying little more than that the women's movement was one of the "signs of the times" to which the Church, along with other institutions, needed to respond. For this bit of wisdom the prelate who delivered the paper in the synod was hailed — even by women — for his insight and sensitivity. And surely he did deserve credit for addressing the subject; but the praise was excessive — the reason being, I suspect, that up to then so little had been said at this level in the Church that even bland remarks seemed rather daring. That would hardly be the case today.

Now, as Lichter-II makes clear, the Church is on the defensive in the media on this subject. The neuralgic case in point is the exclusion of women from the priesthood.

This certainly is not the place to reargue that question. I merely note that, as in the case of clergy sex abuse, so also on this issue, certain underlying attitudes prevalent in the ecclesiastical system have helped exacerbate the situation. I do *not* mean to imply that women should be ordained; I believe that, by the will of Christ, this cannot be done and would not be efficacious — the ordination would not "take" — even if some bishop somewhere did perform the rite on a woman. Rather, I mean that by creating and cultivating a clericalist system, Catholics at all levels and in all states of life — laity as much as clerics — have made the exclusion of women from priestly ordination more controversial and confrontational than it needed to be.

I have written about clericalism in a book called *To Hunt, To Shoot, To Entertain: Clericalism and the Catholic Laity* (Ignatius Press, 1993). The heart of it is the notion that the priesthood is intrinsically superior to every other state in life; that assumption in turn gives rise to unhealthy attitudes regarding superiority and inferiority in the Church, not just among priests but also among lay people.

Clericalism is relevant to the question of women's ordination in at least two ways. First, if it is necessary to be ordained a priest in order to have power and status in the Church, then women interested in having ecclesiastical power and status will want to be ordained. That is why *Media Coverage of the Catholic Church* is on target in treating this topic under the heading "Power Relations." Second, if the priesthood is the highest form of the Christian life — if, one might say, priests get a leg up in the pursuit of sanctity just by being priests — then women who want to live the ideal expression of Christian life and achieve sanctity also will naturally want to be ordained. The result is that, as I pointed out in my book, the women's ordination controversy "will not, and indeed cannot, be settled until the Church comes to grips with clericalism." Add to that the drumbeat of pro-ordination sentiment generated by liberal theologians and publicists, along with the apparent ambivalence of some Church authorities and the reluctance of others to say much about the subject, lest feminists get even angrier, and you have a formula for serious trouble.

But as in the case of sex abuse, so in the case of women's issues, the problem for the Church is further complicated by the attitudes of secular journalists and by the clash of secular and religious cultures. Feminism is a sacred cow in the American newsroom today. This is not to say journalists never report critically on feminism and feminists. But even when they do, journalists take for granted the basic premises and prejudices of the women's movement, its relevance and its fundamental truth, including the truth of its conviction that the Catholic Church is a pervasively patriarchal institution and no friend of women.

Here is one small instance reflecting that. Some years ago, the religion editor of one of the most important daily newspapers in the United States was an ardent feminist, and it showed in her coverage. On one occasion, referring to the Vatican's position on women's ordination, she described it in terms that were not merely superficial but wrong. When I wrote to her about this, she did not trouble to reply, even though we were (I thought) on reasonably good terms. Apparently the matter was not discussable for her — the Church was wrong and that was all there was to it.

The problem here is not a new one. A carefully documented study of what has happened in women's religious institutes in the United States since Vatican Council II — years that have seen the number of religious women fall from about 180,000 in the mid-1960s to fewer than 90,000 by the late 1990s, with their median age rising into the seventies — concludes that the media consistently gave a distorted picture of what was occurring by focusing on advocates of radical change and ignoring religious of a more traditional kind. (See Ann Carey, *Sisters in Crisis: The Tragic Unraveling of Women's Religious Communities,* Our Sunday Visitor, 1997.)

A classic instance occurred in the late 1960s, when Cardinal James McIntyre of Los Angeles and members of the Immaculate Heart of Mary Sisters went head to head over changes in the IHM community. This watershed confrontation, which ended with a large number of the women quitting religious life, set the tone for much that was to come. Throughout, the cardinal was regularly depicted — for example, in *Time* and *Newsweek* — as a reactionary prelate attempting to keep the sisters from carrying out the renewal policies of Vatican Council II. Undoubtedly Cardinal McIntyre was a deeply conservative man who neither understood nor liked what he saw happening in American Catholicism in the late 1960s; but the facts of this episode were different from the media version and by no means as favorable to the sisters and unfavorable to the cardinal as the coverage made it appear.

The IHM sisters were not just good-hearted women trying to comply with Vatican II's directives to renew themselves. Instead, Ann Carey reports that they "went far beyond the guidelines set out by Vatican II and subsequent Church documents relative to religious life. Heavily influenced by the women's liberation movement and the popular psychology of the 1960s, the institute had declared optional virtually all of its past traditions and practices, including common prayer, community life, the religious habit, the corporate apostolate of education, and

127

the shared Eucharist." Yet, even so, the media consistently painted them as "obedient daughters of the Church."

The specifics have changed during the thirty years since then, but the basic reality is the same: People who are critical of the Church's approach to women and demand change can expect sympathetic treatment from the media. In fact, as Lichter-II suggests, things may have gotten worse over the years. One reason lies in the sometimes fumbling efforts of Catholic leadership to deal with the issue. For example, the American bishops' well-intentioned but unsuccessful attempts to agree on a collective pastoral letter on women's concerns — a project that collapsed in the early 1990s after more than nine years of effort — seemed to confirm feminist suspicions while at the same time giving the bishops a black eye.

As for the media, they take it for granted that the Church is mired in patriarchy, just as the feminists say. Many journalists are emotionally, and perhaps intellectually, incapable of grasping the Church's position on the ordination question. Nor does it help that some clergy spend more time apologizing for the position than explaining it, while others imply by winks and nudges — or openly — that the position sooner or later will be abandoned. *Media Coverage* describes the journalistic treatment of the Church and women's issues as "sharply tilted in favor of change." All things considered, it could hardly be otherwise.

Conclusion

What has been said up to this point can be summarized as follows:

• The assimilation of American Catholics into a secular culture hostile to Catholic beliefs and values has done, and goes on doing, serious harm to the Church.

• Elite secular media are an important part of the culture into which Catholics are being assimilated. They transmit its values and serve as its enforcers, rewarding Catholics who conform and penalizing those who do not.

• The two big Catholic stories of the 1990s reported in *Media Coverage of the Catholic Church 1963-1998* reflect that. On clerical sex abuse, the media were expressing the secular culture's antipathy to Catholic sexual morality, especially clerical celibacy. On women's issues, including ordination to the priesthood, the media lined up on the side of feminism against a Church perceived as sexist and patriarchal.

• In regard to both stories, the Church made things harder for itself by various mistakes. The Church cannot afford that in an ideologically hostile media environment.

On the level of fundamental values, the relationship between the media and the Church is essentially adversarial. But the news media in the United States have serious credibility problems of their own, and, in some quarters, their coverage of the Catholic Church is just one more blow to their credibility. In *Breaking the News: How the Media Undermine American Democracy* (Pantheon Books, 1996), journalist James Fallows writes:

> Americans have never been truly fond of their press. Through the last decade, however, their disdain for the media establishment has reached new levels. Americans believe that the news media have become too arrogant, cynical, scandal-minded, and destructive. Public hostility shows up in opinion polls, through comments on talk shows, in waning support for news organizations in their showdowns with government officials, and in many other ways. The most important sign of public unhappiness may be a quiet consumers' boycott of the press. Year by year, a smaller proportion of Americans goes to the trouble of reading newspapers or watching news broadcasts on TV.

For anyone who cares about the role of a free press in a democratic society, this is disturbing. In fact, it is nearly as disturbing as the serious failings of these same media in covering the Church.

The Church cannot save the media. Indeed, it remains to be seen whether it can save itself — at least, in the United States and other Western liberal democracies, where large elements of the Catholic population are thoroughly assimilated into the culture of consumerist secularism. For the Catholic Church to survive in such surroundings as a unified religious community faithful to its own traditions, it will be essential to rebuild a viable Catholic subculture. To some extent, that will mean rebuilding Catholic institutions and programs that now exist — replenishing their diminished sense of Catholic identity and mission. To some extent it will involve creating new institutions and programs in place of old ones that have either disappeared or deteriorated beyond repair.

This is an enormous task. Can it be done? No one really knows. I sometimes refer to what is needed as the "New Ghetto," although that can be misunderstood. I do not mean a return to the Catholic ghetto of the 1940s and 1950s, which, along with all its good qualities, was both too brittle and too superficial to withstand the external and internal shocks of the 1960s and after. The New Ghetto cannot be an ecclesiastical theme park devoted to nostalgic replicas featuring examples of bygone glory days. It must be thoroughly contemporary, in a distinctively *Catholic* way, outward-looking, strong in religious identity and in its determination to form Catholics to engage the secular culture with a view to evangelizing it.

Part of that will involve engaging the secular media. It is often said that in the United States today Catholics are not so much evangelizing the culture as being evangelized by it — won over to its world view and its values. That is eminently true where the media are concerned. Catholics need a serious, workable strategy for evangelizing the media — not that frequently discussed will-o'-the-wisp evangelization *through* media but the rarely discussed yet arguably more urgent work called evangelization *of* media, considered as an aspect of the larger enterprise of evangelizing the culture. There may even be matter here for another study or two.

Russell Shaw is the veteran Washington correspondent of *Our Sunday Visitor* newspaper and is editor of *The Pope Speaks*, a bimonthly documentary periodical. Former secretary of public affairs of the National Conference of Catholic Bishops/United States Catholic Conference, Shaw is the author or coauthor of thirteen books and served as general editor of *Our Sunday Visitor's Encyclopedia of Catholic Doctrine.*

CHAPTER ✦ 5

How to Deal With the Media

BY WILLIAM A. DONOHUE

The survey by the Center for Media and Public Affairs demonstrates the news media's fascination with the Catholic Church's teachings on women and sexuality. Indeed, two thirds of the issues covered by the media address these two subjects. What is driving this fascination is politics.

In their earlier volume, *The Media Elite,* S. Robert Lichter and Linda S. Lichter (along with Stanley Rothman) showed convincingly that the media hierarchy entertain a decidedly left-of-center ideological focus. This orientation tends not to affect reporting when the subject is a purely internal religious matter, such as baptism and confirmation, but it does display itself when controversial "public" issues are involved — for example, the status of women and abortion. In such cases, the degree of scrutiny exercised is almost always microscopic. And it needs to be said that the lens on the microscope is ideologically shaded.

We know from the current study that in half the news stories where the Church's teachings are explained, a dissenting view is proffered. This makes sense given the political cast of mind that is commonplace in the media. It is no secret, after all, that the national news media are clearly supportive of the feminist agenda. Thus, it makes it difficult for them to simply record the Church's positions on women and sexuality; the temptation to seek out a dissenting voice is hard to resist.

What this suggests is something that the Catholic League has long known: When it comes to matters Catholic, the media often go beyond voyeurism and literally seek to change public opinion. That the vector of change is pointing away from the teachings of the magisterium is not surprising given the ideological thrust of the media elite. Thus we learn that 75 percent of the stories on the role of women in the Church urge change or reform, while only 25 percent support current practices.

It is not easy for Catholics to combat bias in the media, and this is especially true when their religion is frequently branded "oppressive." But there are ways to effect change, and that is what this chapter is all about; twelve recommendations for action are offered. Just keep in mind that when it comes to the "hot button" issues of the day, such as women's ordination, abortion, celibacy, and homosexuality, the media bring to the table more than subjectivism: A *preferred* bias, consciously chosen if not always consciously activated, is at work.

1. Organize

It is a lot easier to get your voice heard when you are speaking for a group. This means that you should either start a chapter of an existing organization or start your own. And then get to work sending out news releases registering your concerns.

Forming a chapter of an existing organization is usually not very difficult. Choose an organization that addresses bias in the media, or anti-Catholicism (for example, Catholic League), and request information on starting a chapter. You'll need someone who can spend a little time each week monitoring the media and someone else who can communicate to chapter members the fruits of your labor. This does not entail full-time work, but it does require some work.

Starting your own organization may sound daunting, but it isn't. All you need is an attorney who can file the necessary papers for establishing a nonprofit entity with your state. A nonprofit organization that does not seek to affect the political process is a 501 (c) (3); it is a tax-deductible organization (the Catholic League is such an organization).

You'll also need a phone and a fax. You can use a post office box number for your address and work out of your home. But you have to be accessible to the media and to your members.

Once this is done, you can fax news releases to your local media letting them know the nature of your objections. It is important that you provide evidence of their errors and not just express your anger. The goal is to persuade, not provoke.

If you spot a cartoon in your local newspaper that is offensive, or hear a biased report on TV, you need to act quickly and rationally. If you are writing as an officer of an organization, on letterhead, you will have a much better chance of being taken seriously.

Regarding your letterhead, recruit local notables to be on your board of advisers and then list them on your letterhead. Typically, these will be people who are well-respected by everyone. Don't ask them to do any work for you — simply ask if you can borrow their name for identification purposes. Your goal is to acquire instant standing in your community, and this will certainly help.

2. Coordinate Letter-Writing Campaigns

It is amazing how many people think that letter writing is a waste of time. Yet those in the media know that for every letter they receive from John Doe, there are literally thousands of others who feel the same way. So if you can coordinate a letter-writing campaign, and draw a dozen people to write a letter, the effect will be considerable.

The most read part of any newspaper is the letters-to-the-editor section. By making a few phone calls — and having everyone whom you call do the same — you can quickly seize the moment and create an avalanche effect: The particular offending media won't know what hit them. There is no better way to bring about change than by going directly to the source.

3. Submit Op-Ed Articles

In any organization, you will need someone who can write well. Someone who can cut to the quick. In most newspapers these days, there is an opinion-editorial (op-ed) page that is available for local notables to express themselves in essay form. It is important that someone in your group write a succinct statement that delivers the kind of punch you need to rock the boat a little. You don't need to go ballistic (it won't get printed), but that doesn't mean your only option is to be "non-offensive" (a piece that is too flat will either not get printed or will fail to deliver the desired message).

4. Meet with Editors and Broadcasters

This is a must. No one can be taken seriously if one depends solely on letters and faxes, and this is especially true when dealing with the local media.

There is nothing like a face-to-face meeting with editors and broadcasters. Once your group is up and running, you will be in a position to request such a meeting. What you are aiming for is credibility. This means that you cannot come across either too hard or too soft. It is best to make your points reasonably and forcefully, but without anger. It doesn't hurt to throw in some humor either.

When making your appeals for fairness, be sure to reason by analogy. Anti-Catholicism exists in society for lots of reasons, and sometimes it is so deeply embedded in the offender that he or she isn't fully aware how pervasive it is. Take the ex-altar boy type stories, for instance.

The media thrive on conflict, and when they can't find

enough in real life, they often invent it. A common example is the "Former Altar Boy Mugs Old Lady" type of story. That the mugger is now fifty-eight years of age seems not to matter — that he once was an altar boy is what matters. The point of these references is to say, "See, even good Catholics can be muggers."

In such instances, it is good to ask if the media outlet ever identifies Jewish muggers this way ("Bar-Mitzvahed Boy Mugs Old Lady"). The same thing happens with regard to education. We often see stories that identify a delinquent as being enrolled in a Catholic school, but rarely do we see references made to a delinquent who attends a yeshiva. There is a reason for this and it is called bigotry. Anti-Catholicism, that is.

I once asked some broadcasters who ran an insulting story on the Church whether they had ever run similar shows that exposed wrongdoing in the African American, Native American, Jewish, or gay communities. They hadn't but were without words to explain why. Just to rub it in, I offered a few suggestions of the kinds of topics they might pursue; all dealt with the "dirty laundry" issues that are associated with these groups. They got the point, loud and clear.

The objective of any such meeting is to convince the editors or broadcasters that we Catholics are not offended by fair criticism of the Catholic Church. It is their job, after all, to report the news, and that sometimes means that the news will not be to our liking. What our side should complain about are wild generalizations and stories laced with insult, disdain, and disparagement, not news stories that are simply upsetting to read.

Everyone knows that there are miscreant priests. What matters when such stories are being reported is whether the reporter or commentator takes the next leap and brands all priests that way. If that is done, then the faxes and phone calls should be triggered at once.

Sometimes the story is accurate, but the tone is offensive. TV reporters are especially given to this, and that is why it is important to actually see a tape of the segment in question. Though it can be expensive, in most big cities it is possible to acquire the services of an audiovisual company that tapes virtually all shows. If such a company exists in your area, you can purchase a copy of the tape. Obviously, if you learn of a show that could be a problem before it is aired, be sure to tape it.

5. Start Petition Drives

Petitions can be a very effective vehicle to register a complaint. It takes time, but it is worth the effort.

Choose some issue that you have a reasonably good chance of getting people worked up about and then get them to sign your petition. The petition should target the offending party and should make plain the reasons why you are objecting. If the offense is ongoing, demand that it be discontinued.

Sometimes the focus of a petition will be to seek an apology. If one is forthcoming, but it isn't as strong as you would like it to be, accept it. If you do, you will probably be in a position to secure future apologies from other offending sources. If you don't, you may be labeled unreasonable and won't be taken seriously in the future by new offenders.

If you get a good response, be sure to publicize your efforts. Not only will it bolster the morale of those who signed the petition, it will send a message to would-be offenders that you are serious about having an impact.

6. Place Ads

It's expensive to put an ad in a newspaper, but the results can be significant. A well-written ad that effectively communicates outrage over a news story is attractive to radio and TV outlets. So if they go with it, you get a double hit.

Let's say that your local newspaper continues to misrepresent the truth about something that is important to you. By placing an ad in that newspaper, you are guaranteed to reach its readers, and that alone will infuriate the paper. So what if the newspaper doesn't accept your ad? That's even better, because now you can call a news conference outside the newspaper's offices charging them with spiking your ad solely to protect their backside. Be sure you notify local TV and radio stations about this.

If there are two major newspapers in your area, you might want to place your ad in the opposition newspaper. This can have the effect of bringing other media agents into the picture, thus setting off a wave of news interest. Again, this costs money and therefore it is not something you are likely to do initially. But it is possible that there is some generous, well-to-do person in your community who shares your sentiments and is willing to pick up the tab.

Maybe placing an ad in a newspaper is too expensive or not attractive enough to you. So why not consider placing your ad on public transportation? Putting ads on buses and trains won't be cheap, but it may be more affordable than taking out an ad in a newspaper. Besides, you will likely attract the media to cover your ad campaign as a story.

Don't forget to make use of billboards. In virtually every city, there are heavily traveled highways, intersections, and stopping points where motorists are likely to read a billboard. Most of the billboards feature commercial advertisements. That's why it's a good idea to use this medium for advocacy purposes: Because your ad will be different from the usual fare, everyone will read it.

It can't be said too often that your message must be clear, short, and to the point. Think in terms of sound bites — flashy comments that convey the message with a kick. Remember, you are targeting commuters and therefore must give them something they can instantly understand. It must also be something that will stay with them.

7. Attend Public Hearings

If you are having a persistent problem with a newspaper or TV station, consider holding a public meeting to address the issue. Try to enlist as many notables from other religions to attend as well. Virtually every group now has a Catholic League-type anti-defamation organization that is sensitive to bigotry. If your case is serious enough, you may very well be able to get their support.

The public meeting could take the form of a town hall panel discussion, a civic center conference, a library forum, etc. Perhaps you might want to talk to local public officials as well. While it is not advisable to seek legislation to curb media abuses (this would involve censorship and it is not something that can be recommended), it might help to alert local officials so that they can use their persuasive powers to lobby the media for you.

Depending on the source of the problem, you may want to mobilize your members to buy stock in the offending company and then attend a shareholders meeting. This has been done successfully in the past and is a sure bet to unnerve the culprits. If nothing else, it publicly embarrasses them, and that alone carries weight: They will think twice about offending your group again.

8. Access Talk Radio

Talk radio is one of the most influential sources of communication today. Make sure you send your news releases to every radio station in your area.

Not every station will pick up on your release, but you only need one to get the job done.

If your press statements are summarily ignored, perhaps it is time to consult with someone in the media whom you respect. If that doesn't work, then maybe there is a local writer or journalism professor who is sympathetic to your cause that you could tap for advice. Don't overlook trying to get a meeting with the producer of a local talk-radio show.

If you feel comfortable discussing your issue with an adversary, then let the radio producer know that you are willing and able to debate the subject. This is what talk radio loves and it will make it easier for you to get on the show. But you or whoever it is that represents your group had better be fast on his feet. Having the right instincts isn't good enough.

9. Hold Press Conferences

Holding a press conference can be a great way to get your message across or it can be a bomb. Both the issue you are confronting and the timing of your event are critical. While you are limited in what you can do about the latter, you can do something about the former.

Members of the press get hit with calls and faxes all day long requesting their presence at some event. Therefore, don't bother them until you have established your credibility with the local media. But once you have, you should give it a try.

Conflict attracts the cameras, so be sure to play to this element. Don't wander all over the place — just stick to the issue at hand. If you have some graphics for a backdrop, that can be helpful. Also, consider holding the press conference outside the building of the offending party. And be sure to have some handouts for the press, complete with your name, phone, and fax number.

Regarding the timing of your press conference, try to time it on a day when there isn't a whole lot going on in your area, thus making it more likely that the press will be there. It is best to stage your press conference at some time between midmorning and early afternoon.

10. Stage a Demonstration

You will have to get a lot of people mad at whatever issue is driving you mad before you reach for this weapon. A demonstration that only attracts a few people will be laughed at. But if you can get a few buses full of people, go for it.

You don't need a permit in most places if all you are going to do is march up and down outside a building. But if you are going to tie up traffic or use a bullhorn, then you'll need to get a permit. The best advice is to contact the local authorities and let them know of your event; that way there won't be any problem.

A demonstration provides a great photo opportunity and that is why demonstrations are frequently covered on TV. Be sure you instruct your troops to be orderly. If your group gets obnoxious, you will become the center of unwanted attention, and if that happens, you lose.

11. Boycott Sponsors

It is difficult to boycott the sponsors of a TV news program, simply because it is highly unlikely that offensive segments will be aired night after night. But it may happen that there is a sitcom or drama that is aired nationwide and is offensive to Catholics. Such was the case when ABC aired *Nothing Sacred*. Then it is time for a boycott.

No company wants to needlessly offend a large portion of the public, and that is why boycotts can often be effective. But you need to make sure that when you call for the boycott you have a reasonable chance of succeeding. The show must be sufficiently insulting or disparaging that it provokes a response.

If you learn of a show that has not aired but is slated to be offensive, then you may want to convey to prospective sponsors that if the program is as bad as it is reported to be, then there will be a boycott. We did this with the sponsors of *Nothing Sacred,* and it worked well.

Most advertisers buy a time slot to air their products or services, so when they are confronted with a boycott, they will typically move their money to another time slot. Keep in mind, then, that it makes no sense to "blame" advertisers for airing their commercial during an offensive program; all you want them to do is drop their sponsorship and put their money elsewhere.

12. Develop a Web Page

Once you get up and running, your group will want to contact a computer technician who knows how to develop a web page for you. By posting your activities on the Internet, not only can you get new members, you can activate your current members.

Developing a web page will also give you the legitimacy you need to have clout. It means that the reporters can research your organization from their office, thus providing them with the kind of background information they need to decide whether they should cover your story.

A web page should ideally provide all kinds of tips to members and prospective members. The names and addresses as well as phone and fax numbers of local media should be listed. Over time, you may want to consider archiving materials that the public can access.

Points to Keep in Mind

• Don't forget to thank the media when their coverage is balanced. Otherwise you may be tagged a whiner.

• Don't complain if the reason you're never cited in a story is that you're usually unavailable or don't get back to the media immediately. Reporters work on deadlines so you had better be ready with some rapid-fire responses when they call. Be accessible.

• Don't send your news releases out at the end of the day. If it's too late for the evening news or morning newspapers to interview you, chances are they won't get back to you the next day.

• Don't ever say to a reporter that you can't help him. Make sure you have a good card file system, such as a Rolodex. If you get a call about some issue that you don't have expertise in — or feel uncomfortable with — be sure that you are able to provide a reference. Your Rolodex should contain the names of those who are on your side and who can speak with confidence to the issue. The reporter will remember your help and will likely call you again.

• Don't assume that those in the media hate your side. They don't. Most reporters are primarily concerned with the bottom line, which means they want a story. If you can give them what they need — and fast — they will run with it, no matter how they feel personally. Sure, ideology plays a role (that may be why you're complaining in the first place), but it is also true that once a reporter is on assignment, he or she wants to bring back something that is controversial, something that is newsworthy.

• Don't assume malice is at work when it could be ignorance. Many in the media are not affiliated with any religion and simply don't know a sacrament from a sacrilege. Others are non-Catholics. Some are lapsed, or simply dumb, Catholics. Regardless of what it is, if ignorance is the problem, education is the answer. It is best to provide the offending party with as much credible evidence as you can muster that might change his mind.

• Don't get into the business of questioning motive. It is very difficult, in most instances, to know why someone in the media has offended us, and that is why it is best to just leave this issue alone. If asked by someone in the media whether you are imputing a bad motive to the offender, simply reply that it is the effect, not the intent, that matters. Outcomes count, and in the end it doesn't matter a whole lot whether the offense was intentional or not. What matters is that you, and others, were offended.

• Don't accept the line that the offender can't be guilty because he is a Catholic. Again, what matters is the outcome: If other Catholics are offended, then it doesn't count a whit whether the offender was, or is, a Catholic.

• Don't write a five-hundred-word letter to the editor when the average letter that the newspaper prints is fifty words in length. You would be surprised how many people refuse to abide by this rule. Then they get angry with the newspaper when their letter is not printed, or when it's cut down in size. In short, your letter should be about the average length of what is customarily printed in the newspaper.

• Don't write news releases that go beyond one page. If you do, the second page will likely wind up on the floor or get stuck with some other faxes. First state the facts and then offer a comment.

• Don't forget to let editors and broadcasters know that you know the difference between a news story and an editorial. News stories are supposed to be objective accounts; editorials can offer any point of view. When the former becomes a disguised example of the latter, then that is when you should strike.

Assume the Role of Teacher

Interacting with the media can be a fun experience, and it is doubly fun when you assume the role of teacher. This doesn't mean that you should talk down to the media — on the contrary, a condescending attitude is obnoxious and will not be welcomed — but it does mean that you can often move reporters your way *if* you know what you are talking about and treat the media with the respect they deserve.

For example, when a story about a bad-apple priest elevates to a wild swipe at all priests, then it is time to argue that it is not acceptable journalism to judge a group based on the actions of one person. Provide some examples by discussing the stereotypes of other groups. That usually works.

When dissident Catholics are constantly asked to comment on some Church teaching, ask the reporter whether he feels obliged to seek out a dissident voice in other stories as well. Better yet, come prepared with examples where this game wasn't played, and then ask why. By showing the media that you are tracking them, and are aware of a pattern that is unprofessional, you are in a much better position to force them to reassess what they're doing.

As this survey shows, the media are fascinated with the Church's teachings on women and sexuality; their coverage of these two topics is usually unfavorable. To get at this problem, you might ask reporters why they don't respect house rules. Every organization — and this certainly includes media operations — abides by house rules, strictures that are peculiar to that organization. To outsiders, some of these rules might seem silly, but no one should care as long as membership is voluntary. No one is forced to join the Catholic Church and no one is stopped from leaving. The question remains: Why is it that the media treat Catholicism as if it were different from any other organization?

Perhaps the most fatuous criticism that commonly appears is the rap that Catholicism is authoritarian. Do a little homework and you will find that the Catholic Church tolerates more dissent than any media outlet in the nation. It is not uncommon to read a column by a priest who openly criticizes the Church — in a diocesan newspaper, no less. Yet there isn't a single reporter who regularly slams his newspaper in print or on TV. Nevertheless, it is the Church, not the media, that is branded intolerant.

If you are serious about influencing the media, you might want to consider getting copies of this book into the hands of local reporters, editorial writers, and broadcasters by contacting Our Sunday Visitor at 1-800-348-2440 and asking for *Anti-Catholicism in American Culture*. After you've tapped into some local talent that shares your position, invite the local media to participate in a panel discussion on the survey by the Center for Media and Public Affairs (see Part II, following pages). It could be just the kind of jump-start you need to get going.

William Donahue is president of the Catholic League for Religious and Civil Rights and is the author of three books on civil liberties and contemporary social problems. A leading commentator on Catholicism in the public arena, Donohue holds a Ph.D. in sociology from New York University.

PART

✦

II

CHAPTER 6

Media Coverage of
the Catholic Church —
Executive Summary, 1991 Report

BY LINDA S. LICHTER, S. ROBERT LICHTER, AND DAN AMUNDSON

The public image of social groups and institutions depends heavily on their portrayal in the news media. Given the long history of anti-Catholic prejudice in American society, it is especially important that the media present a fair and balanced portrayal of the Catholic Church. Most journalists approach the Church from an outsider's perspective. A survey of national media outlets indicates that only one to two percent were practicing Catholics. But this need not prevent them from providing fair and balanced coverage of the Church. To address this issue, it is necessary to analyze the style and substance of actual news stories.

To provide an independent assessment of the media's performance, the Knights of Columbus and the Catholic League for Religious and Civil Rights commissioned a scientific study of news coverage by the Center for Media and Public Affairs. The study examined a sample of nationally influential media outlets (*The New York Times, The Washington Post, Time* magazine, and *CBS Evening News*), during three five-year time blocs: 1964-1968, 1974-1978, and 1984-1988. The study focused on

The text in this chapter was originally published by the Knights of Columbus and The Catholic League, © 1991, and was used as the basis for a symposium held in Washington, D.C., to discuss how major U.S. secular media cover the Catholic Church.

both news and editorial material that dealt with Catholic matters, primarily in the United States.

The analysis relied on the social-science method of content analysis. This technique allows researchers to classify the news objectively and systematically, and to produce valid measures of news content. The difference between content analysis and casual monitoring is akin to the difference between scientific polling and man-on-the-street interviews.

Trends in Coverage

On most controversies involving Catholic teachings, the Church came out on the losing side of the issue debate reported in the media. Although the opinion breakdown varied from one issue to another, sources supporting the Church were in the minority on the broad range of debates involving sexual morality and Church authority that dominated the coverage. These included heated controversies over birth control, clerical celibacy, the role of women and minorities in the Church, and its response to internal dissent and issues involving freedom of expression.

The major exception to this pattern involved ecumenical efforts, which the media treated as a kind of "motherhood and apple pie" issue, supported by all people of good will. Even on this dimension, however, opinion was split over whether the Church was helping or hindering efforts to promote interreligious unity. Similarly, opinion was about evenly divided on the Church's involvement in political affairs. But most of the praise was for Church pronouncements condemning war. On domestic disputes over Church-State relations, most sources opposed the Church's positions or activities.

Controversial issues were frequently presented as conflicts between the Church hierarchy, on one side, and lower-level clergy, lay Catholics, and non-Catholics, on the other.

Journalists frequently approached this subject matter from a secular perspective, structuring their coverage of theological issues along the familiar lines of political reportage.

The result was a long-running media drama that pitted a hidebound institutional hierarchy against reformers from within and without. This portrayal was reinforced by the language used to describe the Church in media accounts. The descriptive terms most frequently applied to the Church emphasized its conservative theology, authoritarian forms of control, and anachronistic approach to contemporary society.

Moreover, long-term trends in the coverage have been unfavorable to the Church. Over time, official Church teachings were reported less frequently and were challenged more often when they did appear.

Among the four media outlets in the study, CBS focused most heavily on the papacy and least heavily on social conflicts involving the Church. By contrast, *Time* magazine paid the most attention to dissidents and focused most heavily on conflict, used judgmental language most frequently, and printed more opinions opposed to the Church than favorable on every issue except ecumenism.

Sexual Morality

The Church's teachings on sexual behavior were the leading topic of controversy in every time period and in three of the four outlets in the study. At *The Washington Post*, debate over sexual morals took second place to discussions of power relations within the Church.

Among all statements that clearly expressed their agreement or disagreement with Church teachings on these issues, about four out of seven disagreed with the Church. Church teachings on sexual morality were endorsed almost exclusively by members of the hierarchy; members of the laity and non-

Catholics were overwhelmingly opposed. The overall effect was to present the debate over sexual morality as a split between the Church hierarchy and everyone else.

When discussing Catholic teaching on birth control, 53 percent of sources disagreed with the Church's stand against artificial contraception. As more and more polls indicated that American Catholics were not following the teaching, the subject was relegated to debate within the Church, and news stories rarely quoted opinions from secular sources.

Priestly celibacy was one of the few areas of contention on which opinions did not change much over time, possibly because it was presented entirely as an internal debate among priests and their superiors.

Over time, positions on the Church's opposition to abortion shifted. During the 1970s most published statements supported the Church. This was due to the reiteration of the Catholic teaching by members of the hierarchy in response to the *Roe* v. *Wade* decision. By the 1980s, dissent had nearly doubled; the balance of opinion stood slightly against the Church. This can largely be attributed to secular groups stepping up their campaign for abortion rights and to a group of dissenting nuns and priests who made headlines with a *New York Times* ad requesting a change in Church policy. This prompted the Church to reassert its traditional teaching more frequently.

Church Authority and Dissent

The media gave heavy coverage to issues of power and authority within the Church. Opinions in news stories consistently favored decentralizing power. Support for change was almost twice as frequent as defense of the status quo. Defenders of the status quo were concentrated among the hierarchy. Once again the laity and clergy below the level of bishop lined up on the other side. Among non-Catholics opposition was almost unanimous, at 91 percent.

The Church's traditions came under attack with regard to both its treatment of constituent groups and its handling of dissent. Two out of three sources condemned its handling of dissenters in its ranks, and three out of four criticized its response to issues involving freedom of expression (such as academic freedom at Catholic universities). The only recurrent voices cited in defense of the status quo were again those of the Church hierarchy.

The 1970s saw a dramatic change in this arena of debate. Women's rights and status became the major point of contention. As racism and sexism loomed larger in debate, the Church was often attacked by secular sources.

The most dramatic rise in discussion during the 1980s came in the area of free expression. This was largely due to discussions of academic freedom and dissent connected to such high-profile figures as Father Charles Curran and Archbishop Raymond Hunthausen, along with Cardinal Joseph Ratzinger's push for greater theological orthodoxy. In this area Church decisions were rejected or criticized in 63 percent of all opinions.

Ecumenism and Church-State Relations

Overall, seven out of ten sources supported Church efforts to build unity and improve relations with other world religions. Even so, when debate arose over the Church's position on this widely approved goal, half the sources criticized the Church as an obstacle to greater unity.

Discussions of the Catholic Church's relations with various levels of government in the United States received the least coverage of any dimension in this study. Opinion was about evenly split, with 51 percent supporting the Church in its relations with government and 49 percent expressing some criticism. Over the course of time, however, opinion clearly turned against the Church. By the 1980s, those who supported the Church had dropped to a minority of only 40 percent.

Support for the Church's relations with the political world was bolstered by the Church's anti-war stance. On domestic concerns, by contrast — concerns such as public funding for private schools, the politics of abortion legislation, and perceived threats to the separation of Church and State — few sources supported Church involvement in political affairs.

Church involvement in politics was always seen as an inappropriate threat to the separation of Church and State. The margin of criticism increased in recent years. In the 1970s, critics outnumbered supporters by a two-to-one margin, and in the 1980s the margin widened to three-to-one.

Descriptive Language

The media's depiction of the Church includes not only its presentation of policy issues but also the tone of news accounts, which is strongly influenced by the use of descriptive language. A majority of stories employing descriptive language stressed the Church's conservatism, in all outlets and time periods studied. The tendency to emphasize the Church's conservatism increased during the 1970s. In addition, the Church was overwhelmingly portrayed as an oppressive or authoritarian institution. Over the course of time the Church was increasingly portrayed in this light. An institution that was usually described as conservative and oppressive was also presented more often than not as irrelevant. The Church's lack of relevance was emphasized more heavily in recent years. In sum, the linguistic tone of news coverage has been generally (and increasingly) unfavorable to the Church. At every outlet, and during every time period, it was usually portrayed as an oppressive or authoritarian institution with little relevance for the contemporary world.

Ultimately, journalists are less fact-collectors than story-tellers. And the stories they tell about the Catholic Church rely on politics as much as religion for their dramatic appeal. Increasingly, the story line revolves around a beleaguered authority struggling to enforce its traditions and decrees on a reluctant constituency.

CHAPTER ✧ 7

Media Coverage of the Catholic Church 1963-1998

By Linda S. Lichter, S. Robert Lichter, and Dan Amundson

Executive Summary

How do the news media portray the Catholic Church? Has their portrayal changed over the past several decades? If so, in what ways does current coverage differ from that of the past? To answer these questions, the Catholic League for Religious and Civil Rights and Our Sunday Visitor commissioned the Center for Media and Public Affairs (CMPA) to conduct a scientific content analysis of leading print and broadcast news outlets during the 1990s. This represents an updating of CMPA's 1991 study, *Media Coverage of the Catholic Church,* which was sponsored by the Catholic League and the Knights of Columbus.

For the new study, we examined 569 news items that appeared from 1994 through 1998 on the ABC, CBS, and NBC evening newscasts; in *Time, Newsweek,* and *U.S. News & World Report;* and in *The New York Times, The Washington Post,* and *USA Today.* We compared the results to our previous study of 1,876 news items that appeared from 1964 through 1988 in *The New York Times, The Washington Post, Time,* and *CBS Evening News.*

Major Findings: In the 1990s

• The role of women in the Church was the leading source of controversy. This was debated more frequently than all issues involving Church-State relations and Church teachings on sexual morality combined.

• Three out of four sources criticized the Church's treatment of women. Over 90 percent of sources on TV news were critical of the Church.

• Criminal charges against clerics — especially allegations of pedophilia — accounted for one out of every twelve discussions about the Catholic Church.

• Seven out of ten sources criticized the way the Church handled charges of criminal wrongdoing.

• Nine out of ten sources criticized the Church's ecumenical efforts. Catholic-Jewish relations were a particular focus of concern.

• Overall, the media debate was balanced on issues involving Church-State relations and teachings on sexual morality, such as abortion and clerical celibacy. But there were significant differences among media outlets.

• TV news paid the most attention to sexual issues and was most critical of Church doctrine in this area. *USA Today* paid the most attention to charges of wrongdoing against clerics.

Changes Over Time

• The amount of coverage of the Catholic Church declined by over 50 percent from the 1960s to the 1990s.

• Criminal allegations against clerics emerged as a major topic of discussion in the 1990s.

• Overall, Church teachings and practices received less support in the 1990s than in any previous decade.

• Debate over power relations within the Church surged, while debate over Church doctrine on sexual morality declined.

• Support for reform of Church authority structures rose to new highs. Fewer than one out of three sources supported the current distribution of power.

• The Church was usually described as a conservative

institution, but the use of ideological labels declined over time.

* * *

National media coverage of the Catholic Church continues to revolve around questions of power and authority. That parallels the media's treatment of political news. This perspective emphasizes the intersection of Church doctrine with secular political controversies, as well as the distribution of power among constituent groups. In the 1990s, the Church was portrayed as a conservative institution that should grant more authority to women, respond more aggressively to wrongdoing by its representatives, and improve its relations with other religions. Although the particular topics of concern have changed over time, the tendency to portray controversies involving the Church in terms of their political significance has remained constant.

Introduction

In 1991, the Catholic League for Religious and Civil Rights and the Knights of Columbus commissioned the Center for Media and Public Affairs to study major media coverage of the Catholic Church in America from the 1960s through the 1980s. To accomplish this, we employed content analysis, a social science technique that allows researchers to classify news items objectively and systematically. We analyzed a sample of 1,876 news and editorial items from over ten thousand that appeared on CBS, in *The New York Times, The Washington Post,* and *Time* magazine. This study compared not only changes in coverage over time but also variations among these major media outlets.

Our analysis included the frequency and nature of topics, such as routine Church events, news about the pope, dissent within the Church, its relations with other religions, its role in politics, and its positions on abortion, birth control, and civil rights. We categorized all viewpoints expressed on these topics and all sources cited in stories, from members of the Church hierarchy and lay Catholics to external groups and government representatives. We not only documented the nature of these sources but the types of issues they addressed. Beyond these essential elements of coverage, we investigated how often official Church teachings were cited and whether they were challenged by critics.

After examining the factual elements contained in news accounts, we analyzed their tone as well through the language used to describe the Church and its teachings. These rhetorical labels identified the Church's political ideology, its structure, and its relevance in the modern world.

This study generated widespread debate about the depth and fairness of the media's coverage of the Church. Many Catholics believe journalists harbor an anti-Catholic bias that is reflected in their stories, which distort the Church's true character. In contrast, journalists maintain that they adhere to their professional code of fairness and balance in reporting on the Church, even though most are outsiders and have a secular perspective. Ultimately, it is their coverage, not their personal beliefs, that determines how the Catholic Church is treated.

Recently, the Catholic League and Our Sunday Visitor asked us to update this study to determine if coverage had changed in the 1990s. We expanded the research base to include all three network evening newscasts (not just CBS). Despite the explosive growth of cable news stations in the last few years, the three major networks remain the most influential sources of televised news. Likewise, we extended our analysis of weekly newsmagazines from *Time* to *Newsweek* and *U.S. News & World Report* as well. Finally, we added *USA Today* to our newspaper sample. While *The New York Times* and *The Washington Post* serve as opinion leaders for journalists in America, *USA Today* has become a national newspaper for a broad-based audience. The current study examined 569 news items from over three thousand appearing during this decade.

Ongoing events and new controversies have kept the Catholic Church in the news during the 1990s. While the media continue to chronicle the pope's extensive travels, current coverage is notable for its attention to alleged crimes by clerics, especially pedophilia, a topic absent from past coverage. For example, allegations made and later retracted regarding Cardinal Joseph Bernardin captured headlines during the last years of his life. Among other new subjects that framed news coverage of the Church in the 1990s were scientific advances in artificial reproduction, shifts in the Church population, and challenges to the limited roles of Catholic women.

We will present our findings for media coverage of the Church in the 1990s, then compare these results to those of the previous three decades. For purposes of uniformity, we restricted our historical comparisons to outlets used for the original study. While the present analysis is self-contained, a fuller appreciation of this subject requires the reading of the original study as well.

Amount of Coverage

To analyze media coverage of the Catholic Church, we concentrated on a sample of nationally influential news outlets: *The New York Times, The Washington Post,* and *USA Today,* which are the nation's most influential general interest daily newspapers; *Time, Newsweek,* and *U.S. News & World Report,* the most widely read general interest weekly newsmagazines; and the evening newscasts of ABC, CBS, and NBC, which are the nation's most frequently watched broadcast news programs. These outlets serve as opinion leaders for both the general public and the journalistic profession. This sample represents a considerable expansion of our previous sample, which was limited to the *Times* and *Post, Time,* and CBS. Therefore, as we note below, our analysis of historical trends will be limited to the four outlets that were examined in both studies.

As in our previous study, we selected a five-year period from 1994-1998, corresponding to the mid-decade time block examined in earlier decades. We focused on news items that dealt with the Catholic Church in the United States. For example, the sample included news about policy statements by the Vatican that would affect American Catholics, but not news that focused primarily on the Church's role in other countries. We defined news items to include both news and editorial pieces, but not letters to the editor.

During the five-year period that we studied, the nine national news outlets produced 3,103 news items regarding the Catholic Church. Some 90 percent of these (2,820) appeared in the three newspapers, and the majority (1,778) appeared in *The New York Times* alone. Therefore, to create a more manageable but still representative sample, we took 10 percent random samples of all newspaper articles, in addition to all stories that appeared in the newsmagazines or on the network evening news shows. This procedure produced an overall sample of 569 news items, which included 180 *New York Times* articles, 79 *Washington Post* articles, and 27 *USA Today* articles; 30 pieces in *Time* magazine, 21 in *Newsweek,* and 16 in *U.S. News & World Report;* 77 stories broadcast on ABC, 69 on CBS, and 70 on NBC. (See Table 1.)

The sheer number of news stories that we coded is itself significant in understanding the image of the Catholic Church that the news audience receives. For example, readers of *The*

New York Times would have seen, on average, nearly a story per day on the Church, over twice the volume of coverage to which *The Washington Post* readers were exposed. The *Post,* in turn, published three times as many stories about the Church as did *USA Today*. In fact, the disparity between America's most "elite" national newspaper (*The New York Times*) and the only truly national paper aimed at a general audience (*USA Today*) is remarkable. Whereas the *Times* averaged nearly one story per day, *USA Today* published barely one per week.

The disparity in coverage among newspapers stands in sharp contrast to the other news genres that we sampled. *Time* published about twice as many stories on the Church as did *US News* (30 versus 16), straddling *Newsweek*'s total of 21 stories. The networks were even more similar in the amount of coverage they devoted to the Church, with only a trivial number of stories separating the leader (ABC) from its two competitors (CBS and NBC). In this case, however, it was the absence of differences that proved noteworthy. ABC attracted considerable attention when it hired the first religion beat reporter on a network news show. Nonetheless, ABC devoted about the same level of attention to the Catholic Church as did the other networks. In terms of airtime, ABC led with 1 hour 53 minutes, only 8 minutes ahead of NBC's 1 hour 45 minutes, with CBS lagging behind at 1 hour 29 minutes. Over a five-year period, differences of this magnitude are trivial.

Topics

By far, the largest number of stories about the Catholic Church were straightforward accounts of predictable and relatively noncontroversial occurrences, such as announcements of parish events, promotions of clergy, and the accomplishments of outstanding Catholics. (See Table 2.) In our sample, such "Church happenings" were the subject of 239 stories, over a third (34 percent) of the entire sample. For example, *The New York Times* profiled how the destruction and resurrection of an old church affected the congregation:

> The parishioners of St. Philip Neri Roman Catholic Church stood shoulder to shoulder in June and wept. Octogenarian descendants of Italian immigrants and teenagers from the Dominican Republic watched in horror as flames consumed their century-old church in the Bedford Park section of the Bronx.
>
> Six months later, the majestic arches of a new roof are sprouting from a maze of construction scaffolding inside the church's sanctuary. To the delight of St. Philip Neri officials, more than $700,000 of the $1 million needed to reconstruct the historic building already lies in church coffers.
>
> Donations from former parishioners, graduates of the church's elementary school, other churches and sympathetic strangers have poured in from across the city, the region and the world. Contributions ranging from a crumpled dollar bill to a corporate check for $100,000 have arrived continually at the 3,000-member church since the fire, which was caused by an electrical spark on June 15. . . .
>
> Parishioners said the drive to rebuild the church, which was built by Italian laborers in 1899, has created a sense of commonality in the parish of elderly Italians and Irish and young Latinos, blacks and Koreans.
>
> — *The New York Times,* January 5, 1998, p. B3

Such coverage did not necessarily reflect positively on the Church, as the following *Washington Post* story illustrates:

166

The Vatican permitted scrutiny of one of the most notorious periods in Roman Catholic Church history, opening its archives of the Inquisition and showing that even some versions of the Bible were once blacklisted. Scholars now will be able to study cases such as that of the astronomer Galileo, condemned by the Inquisition for claiming the Earth revolved around the Sun, and Giordano Bruno, a monk burned for heresy in 1600 in Rome's Campo dei Fiori square.

Also opened was the infamous Index of Forbidden Books that Catholics were forbidden to read or possess on pain of excommunication. It showed that non-Latin versions of the Bible were on the blacklist because the church was suspicious of allowing access to sacred texts without ecclesiastical guidance.

— *The Washington Post,* January 23, 1998, p. A30

News about the pope's activities and pronouncements accounted for another 99 stories or one out of every seven (14 percent) in the sample. Thus, coverage of the Church's spiritual leader and the aspects of its daily functioning accounted for nearly half of all news coverage (48 percent). In the current decade, the media noted all signs of the pope's failing health. For example, on January 19, 1998, Andrea Mitchell gave the following chronology on *NBC Nightly News:* "July 15, 1992, he suffered the removal of a precancerous tumor and gall bladder surgery, November 1993 a dislocated shoulder, April 1994 hip replacement, October 1996 appendectomy and now what is assumed to be Parkinson's disease, according to a neurologist at Georgetown University."

But much of this coverage simply recounted the schedules and particulars of papal appearances, as in this *Newsweek* piece:

This week, on his fourth — and quite likely last — visit to the United States, the pope will address the United Nations on its 50th anniversary. It will also be 30 years to the day that Paul VI became the first pope to visit the United States and to address the United Nations. . . .

In his five-day sweep, John Paul II will say four outdoor masses — two at sports stadiums, one at a racetrack and one in New York's Central Park. He'll pray with President Bill Clinton in Newark, N.J., meet with rabbis and other religious leaders in New York City and parade through Baltimore.

— *Newsweek,* October 9, 1995, p. 63

Such stories typically form a noncontroversial backdrop against which more conflictual or controversial stories stood out in sharp relief. Paramount among these was the category of crimes by clerics. Allegations of wrongdoing, such as sexual abuse by priests, made up the third most frequent category of stories about the Church, accounting for one in every twelve news items (8 percent) over the entire five-year period. Typically, they involved the exploitation of underage males by priests. Some stories focused on a particular case. For example, Forrest Sawyer of *ABC World News Tonight* reported on July 17, 1998: "In Stockton, California, a jury awarded two brothers who were molested by a priest $30 million in damages from the Catholic diocese. They said the diocese tried to conceal the fact that their family priest, Rev. O'Grady, had a history of abusing children."

One NBC report by Andrea Mitchell examined the issue from a broader financial perspective, noting that thousands of such sexual abuse cases were pending across the country. The damages sought in one were $500 million. Mitchell said that since 1986, some insurers have excluded sexual abuse from their policies. Actual damages paid were difficult to estimate, according to a spokesman from the National Conference of Bishops that she interviewed. "The church has paid under $100 million. There is no requirement that churches or dioceses report either suits or settlements, so we are only guessing" (December 7, 1994).

A *Time* piece also explored this issue extensively, from the salacious details of sexual abuse to how the Church deals with offenders:

> Over a period of 14 years, Father John Hanlon of St. Mary's in Plymouth, Massachusetts, would occasionally take boys under his charge to a nude beach. It was, a lawyer would later claim, the parish priest's way "to desensitize" them to their own nakedness. Hanlon, however, would subject his wards to more dissolute initiations. He sexually abused 10 of them, ranging in age from 12 to 15, including William Wood, now 27. . . . Hanlon, now 65, denied the charges, but last week a jury in Plymouth County found the priest guilty, and he was sentenced to three concurrent life terms for the rape of Wood. . . . The harsh judgment on Hanlon is only the latest chapter in a plague of lawsuits that is bedeviling the Roman Catholic Church in America. "Roderick MacLeish Jr., a Boston lawyer involved in civil action [dealings] against alleged child abusers, claims that of the 400 active cases handled by his firm, 250 involve clergy — and the vast majority of them belong to the Catholic Church.
>
> "Over the last few years, the Church has been forced to pay out tens of millions of dollars in fines and settlements. Meanwhile, if they are not subjects of criminal investigation, most fallen priests are sent into therapy

and are either retired or dispatched to posts that do not put them into regular contact with children." The diocese-by-diocese approach has created a label of reactions. Rather than go into the problem piecemeal, says Lisa Cahill, professor of ethics at Boston College's theology department, "the missing piece is for the Church to take responsibility as an institution." At the moment, however, Rome considers pedophilia a local American problem.

— *Time,* May 9, 1994, p. 56

All other topics that accounted for more than 2 percent of the coverage likewise concerned issues that involved controversy and conflict. They include the role of the Church in American politics (6 percent of all stories); and the changing nature of the Church population, such as the substantial growth of a Catholic Hispanic community; disputes over canon law, the official body of Church teachings; and the continuing debate over the Church's position on abortion, each of which accounted for an additional 5 percent of the coverage.

Among these issues, the most diffuse involved the Church's role as a religious body operating in the political realm. A 1997 *New York Times* profile of John M. Smith, the new bishop of Trenton, New Jersey, illustrated his concern over the Church's ability to sustain programs for the poor without sufficient government assistance:

> Churches are providing services that are the province of the government. Inner-city Catholic schools provide a quality education to many non-Catholics. Besides education, there's alcoholic treatment, shelters for abused wives, relieving the strife of poor people. The Catholic church, to its credit, never abandoned the inner cities.

But we can't do it without state and Federal funding. We're going to encourage Catholics to exercise their vote in elections, to lobby for funding. Catholic schools, with 52,000 students, save taxpayers millions. Vouchers would help us very much.

— *The New York Times,* June 22, 1997, p. 13NJ

Changes in the character of the Church's population discussed both the clergy and the laity. NBC noted the Church's growth in Hispanic areas of the country. For example, the pastor of St. Francis of Assisi in San Jose, California, observed that "three years ago when I came here, we had 300 families for the parish. Now we have 700 families and we gained 120 families in the last six months" (*NBC Nightly News,* June 28, 1997).

A more extensive piece by *U.S. News & World Report* examined the problem created by the growth of the Church population and the drastic decline of available priests:

Martin Luther once described his ideal church as a "priesthood of all believers," where God and the faithful could commune without the intercession of a priest. Ironically, the Roman Catholic Church is now moving toward a variation on that vision — not out of theological conviction but because it is deep in the throes of a clerical shortfall. More than 2,000 American parishes — about 11 percent — now lack a resident priest and must be served by circuit riders.

While the ranks of the Catholic faithful in the United States have swelled from 45 million to 60 million since 1965, the number of priests has shrunk from 58,632 to 49,551. And many of those are retired or inactive. Sociologists Richard Schoenherr and Lawrence Young have estimated that in 1975 there were 1,102 lay Catholics for every active priest. By 1995, the ratio was 1,797 to 1. Many parishes are so strapped that laypeople now do everything from handling business matters to distributing Communion wafers previously consecrated by a priest.

— *U.S. News & World Report,* December 30, 1996/January 6, 1997

Canon law is an esoteric subject rarely discussed in the general media. But it was prominently featured last year when Bill Clinton violated one of its rules:

President Clinton took Holy Communion during a South African Mass late last month at the invitation of the local priest, White House officials said today in response to criticism that giving Communion to Mr. Clinton, a Baptist, violated Roman Catholic doctrine.

Mr. Clinton never receives Communion in Catholic churches in the United States. But Tarry Toiv, a White House spokesman, said the priest, Father Mohlomi Makobane, told White House staff members before Mr. Clinton's visit to his Soweto church that "this was the policy of the South African Conference of Bishops, that Communion was open to non-Catholics."

No such lenient policy exists, the Southern African bishops declared late last week. In January, however, the bishops did issue rules that allow non-Catholics to receive Communion in certain special circumstances, and the Vatican has requested clarification of that policy.

— *The New York Times,* April 7, 1998, p. A20

The importance of who may participate in the Eucharist was emphasized by the Vatican's involvement in this event and disputes over the interpretation of Church doctrine. The same *New York Times* story noted:

> The president's decision to receive Communion prompted church officials from South Africa to the Vatican to the United States to declare in recent days that Father Makobane had misinterpreted church doctrine.
>
> "The action taken by the priest in South Africa, however well-intended, was legally and doctrinally wrong in the eyes of the church law and church doctrine," Cardinal John O'Connor, the archbishop of New York, said in a Palm Sunday sermon.
>
> Explaining that he was trying to address confusion among Catholics caused by the news of the incident, the Cardinal said: "Some undoubtedly believe that if one has enough prestige or money, anything goes." The church, he said, should not contribute to such perceptions.
>
> — *The New York Times,* April 7, 1998, p. A20

The Church has been a consistent if minor player in news about one of this country's most divisive issues — abortion. The international ramifications of its position were highlighted by the following front-page story:

> After a day of tortuous closed-door talks that pitted Vatican diplomats against many other delegates, the United Nations population conference failed tonight to reach a compromise on the contentious issue of abortion.
>
> Standing alone, Vatican diplomats blocked a consensus on a formula sponsored by Pakistan, saying they found it unacceptable. The proposed formula itself took five hours of haggling among 15 countries. . . .

The move by the Vatican reflected Pope John Paul II's ardent crusade against abortion. But many delegates have noted that abortion is only one element of the far broader issue facing the meeting — averting a disaster in global population growth.

— *The New York Times,* September 7, 1994, p. A1

Another article in *The Washington Post* demonstrated the diverse political issues connected to promoting the Church's pro-life position:

America's top Catholic leaders yesterday launched an aggressive new campaign to lobby against abortion and to mobilize parishes across the country into a powerful new voting bloc against candidates who support abortion rights.

The bold assertion by the nation's Catholic bishops marks a new era in the church's political activism. While the church's 400 bishops have always strongly opposed abortion, many have been reluctant to impose their views in a public arena. Not since the 1970s have they vowed as a group to so directly and visibly influence politicians and voters on such a critical issue.

— *The Washington Post,* November 19, 1998, p. A1

The long-standing debate between science and religion as it pertains to the Church accounted for another 4 percent of all stories. *The New York Times* sketched the outlines of John Paul's thinking on this subject in an article entitled "The Philosopher Pope":

The powerful encyclical issued last week by Pope John Paul II . . . is a missive from a religious philosopher to the world's intelligentsia. It is a plea for an end to the separation of faith and reason and an argument against the "philosophy of nothing," as he calls the various forms of nihilism that have taken root in a war-weary century.

Written for the bishops of the Catholic Church, the decree, called "Fides et Ratio" (Faith and Reason), argues that these two strains of human endeavor need not exclude each other in the pursuit of truth. Science and rational thought do not wipe out the exploration of "the fundamental questions which pervade human life," as John Paul writes. Similarly religion, especially Catholicism, needs the pursuit of rational debate to keep such spiritual matters from "withering into myth or superstition. . . ."

The pope also wants to bring the questions of morality back into the pursuit of science — an issue that at once seems as medieval as Galileo and as modern as Hiroshima. If science does not move beyond the utilitarian, he argues, it could "soon prove inhuman and even become the potential destroyer of the human race."

— *The New York Times,* October 21, 1998, p. A24

The New York Times also noted the Church's involvement in another science-related controversy — cloning:

Cardinal O'Connor said that the joining of a man and a woman is the proper way to create human life, and that cloning perverts that process. "It is a drastic invasion of human parenthood," the Cardinal said. "This does disrespect both to the dignity of human procreation and the dignity of the conjugal union."

The Cardinal also said he wondered if human cloning might result in the production of people for the purposes of warfare or slavery.

—*The New York Times,* March 14, 1997, p. B2

Catholic relations with other religions, the role of women in the Church, and how the Church treated dissenters each accounted for an additional 3 percent of the coverage. Exemplifying the severest consequences for dissent was a *Washington Post* piece on one of the most controversial actions by a Catholic official during this decade:

> A little-known bishop in Lincoln, Neb., has sent shock waves through the Roman Catholic Church by threatening to excommunicate Catholics in his diocese by May 15 if they do not resign from a dozen groups he deems "totally incompatible with the Catholic Faith."
>
> The forbidden groups include several challenging church teaching on abortion, birth control or the ban on female priests. But one group — Call to Action, a Chicago-based group promoting church reform — counts among its members thousands of priests and nuns and several American bishops.
>
> — *The Washington Post,* July 11, 1995, p. A1

While the role of women in the Church is sometimes covered as a form of dissent, we separately coded the broader category of women's issues. This 1995 *Washington Post* article illustrates the fine but firm line the pope draws on this subject:

> Pope John Paul II issued a manifesto on women's rights today, putting himself on the side of equal treatment and apologizing for past discrimination in the Ro-

man Catholic Church, but reaffirming the ban on women priests.

In a 19-page letter addressed to "women throughout the world," the pope went so far as to praise women's liberation as "substantially a positive" process, despite what he termed "mistakes," while holding firm to Roman Catholic teachings on issues such as priesthood and abortion that long have been bones of contention between feminists and the church hierarchy.

The latter summed up several weeks of papal utterances on women's issues in advance of the U.N. conference on women scheduled for September in Beijing. The Vatican, conservative on issues of sex and birth control and opposed to abortion and the expansion of gender definition to include homosexuality, has been gearing up for a possible conflict at the China meeting with secular feminists.

— *The Washington Post,* March 29, 1996, p. A3

Rounding out the top dozen topics (with 2 percent of the coverage) was education, with special reference to the role of Catholic schooling in America. These dozen topics together accounted for 93 percent of all coverage of the Catholic Church in the national news media.

Just as variations in the amount of coverage tell us something about the differing approach that various news organizations took to the Catholic Church, so did the topics on which their coverage focused. Television's coverage was concentrated on what might be called "official" news. This medium produced the heaviest coverage of the pope, who provides good visuals on his many papal visits around the globe, as well as the catchall institutional category that we termed "Church happenings." These two categories together accounted for almost two thirds (64 percent) of all television news coverage of the Catholic Church. This concentration of coverage of institutional activities dwarfed that of any other outlet in the sample. For example, the number of stories in our *New York Times* sample nearly equaled that of the three networks combined. Yet the 180 *Times* articles that we analyzed included only 9 discussions of the pope's activities compared to 65 out of the 216 television news stories.

Conversely, and perhaps unexpectedly, television news paid relatively little attention to the Church's role in some hot button political controversies. For example, the networks devoted proportionately less coverage than did other outlets to the Church and the abortion issue, civil rights, the role of women, and birth control. (Our analysis covers only the intersection of these issues with the Catholic Church, not the total coverage of the issues themselves.)

Perhaps equally surprising was the outlet that paid the most attention (as a proportion of its overall coverage) to the intersection of religion and politics. It was *USA Today,* which devoted fully one sixth (17 percent) of its coverage to the Church's role in the political system:

> St. Peter Church is a commanding presence in downtown Boerne, Texas, its twin towers looking down over the historic center of the city in the hill country near San Antonio.
>
> When the Roman Catholic Archdiocese announced plans to demolish most of the seventy-year-old church, city officials invoked historic preservation laws to stop the project.
>
> The zoning dispute might have remained intensely local, but it got caught up in a constitutional argument over the relationship between the courts, local govern-

ments, and religious practices and institutions. Now the Supreme Court has agreed to hear the case early next year in a move that could redefine the relationship between Church and State.

The Texas dispute took on national dimensions when the archdiocese invoked a newly passed federal law in its fight to keep the city from interfering with its demolition plans.

The 1993 Religious Freedom Restoration Act was aimed at encouraging governments to accommodate religious practices. In effect, the law tells federal courts how to weigh disputes that arise when governments seek to enforce general laws in ways that impinge on religion.

— *USA Today,* October 16, 1996, p. A3

USA Today also paid the most attention to the Church's role in the politics of abortion — 10 percent of its coverage, double the overall average. For example, one article recounted a cardinal's call to halt protests at abortion clinics:

A cardinal's plea for a moratorium on protests at abortion clinics has slowed but hasn't stopped the demonstrations. . . .

Law, who has urged activists to take their prayer vigils off the streets and into churches, is in the forefront of a movement by moderate abortion-rights opponents to end violence.

— *USA Today,* January 11, 1995, p. A2

Such coverage came at the expense of a focus on the more traditional institutional functioning of the Church. *USA Today* devoted by far the least attention to Church happenings, only one tenth of its total coverage, compared to nearly two fifths of the coverage in both *The New York Times* and the television news shows. Thus, our newspaper samples produced eighty-two stories on Church happenings in *The New York Times* compared to a mere three stories in *USA Today*.

Other areas of social controversy proved to be a specialty of *The Washington Post*. The *Post* produced the heaviest coverage of crimes by clerics (13 percent versus 8 percent overall), dissent in the Church (7 percent versus 3 percent overall), and women's issues (6 percent versus 3 percent overall). Dissent is a natural subject for the *Post,* because the structure of political news requires referencing critics of a given law, policy, or proposal. The prominence of the women's issue is a function of coverage of legislation that affects women across the country, as well as the presence of prominent women's groups and individuals in Washington, D.C.

Among the stories on clerical wrongdoing in the *Post* was the following account of a priest charged with molesting altar boys:

> The Roman Catholic Diocese of Dallas agreed yesterday to pay $23 million to eight former altar boys who were sexually abused for years by a priest, by far the largest settlement the Catholic Church has ever been forced to reach in such a case. . . .
>
> The Catholic Church has been besieged in the last decade with cases of sexual abuse of minors by priests — more than 200 of them have been jailed for that offense since the 1980s — but few are more extensive than the one in Dallas involving Rudolph "Rudy" Kos.
>
> Kos has been convicted of molesting altar boys and several other youths over a period of 11 years in three church parishes. The victims accused Kos of hundreds of incidents of sexual abuse, beginning for some of the

boys when they were as young as 9 years old. The abuse ranged from genital massages to forced oral sex, and at times also including drugs and alcohol.

— *The Washington Post,* July 11, 1998, p. A1

A *Post* piece on dissent in the Church involved reaction to the Vatican's threat to punish those who challenged its teachings:

> Liberal Catholic scholars reacted yesterday with surprise and disappointment to a formal decree by Pope John Paul II that church theologians who break with Catholic teachings on such subjects as euthanasia, sex outside marriage and the ordination of women could face punishment.

> While the Vatican has always asserted its authority on these controversial issues, the pope's latest document reinforces the church's ability to enforce its rules by encoding these teachings in canon law, the core beliefs of Roman Catholics. Church leaders will now find it easier to discipline dissenters with what the pope called "just punishment," which can mean anything from a temporary suspension from teaching duties to excommunication.

> The pope's sudden decision to clarify and solidify the church's position reflects one of his first attempts to lay down a lasting legacy for his papacy. At a time when a growing number of Catholics, particularly in America, are challenging church teachings, John Paul wants to quiet the voices of liberal Catholics who dissent from essential dogmas.

> But many of the university teachers and other theologians who are the chief target of the pope's order said

John Paul's decision would only increase the divisive-
ness. . . .

— *The Washington Post,* July 2, 1998, p. A1

The Washington Post also investigated women's issues.
The following example examined the possible reasons for the
decline of women religious:

> Specialists differ on why young women are not
> joining religious orders. The Rev. Andrew W. Greeley, a
> Catholic sociologist, speculated about several possibili-
> ties in his book "The Catholic Myth." They include the
> "emancipation" of the orders, which lead to a removal of
> the rigid life that appealed to some members.
>
> Perhaps, he said, younger women no longer see any-
> thing unique in the vocations of nuns that could not be
> achieved in lay ministries.

— *The Washington Post,* February 26, 1994, p. B7

Not surprisingly, considering that it serves the nation's capital, the *Post* also devoted an above average proportion of its coverage to the Church's role in politics: 10 percent of its total coverage. That is well below *USA Today*'s 17 percent, but double the
5 percent that we recorded in *The New York Times* and the television networks. A 1997 *Post* piece explored the Church's opposition to physician-assisted suicide initiatives in various states:

> [A conference] of bishops in Maryland, the Dis-
> trict and Wilmington, Del., is working with hospice or-
> ganizations and other groups to introduce a bill in Mary-
> land that would outlaw physician-assisted suicide. The
> bill would be introduced when the General Assembly
> reconvenes in January.

How much of a role religion will play in renewed local debates on physician-assisted suicide is unclear. Thus far, the antireligion rhetoric seen in Oregon — particularly against the Catholic Church — has not been seen in this area, despite the local church's "high visibility" in opposition to assisted suicide. . . .

The Catholic Church opposed assisted suicide based on its reading of Scripture, on centuries of tradition and on reason. . . . And it believes in a "natural law" that tells any person instinctively that certain acts are wrong, such as stealing, committing murder or taking one's life. Natural law derives from God's law, which is God's will, and takes precedence over human laws.

— *The Washington Post,* November 15, 1997, p. B8

Sources

If the topics of discussion tell us what the news is about, the sources who are quoted tell us which voices are heard. To ascertain who supplied the information for these stories, we identified every named source in every story who provided information or commentary for the news. This resulted in 2,242 identifiable source references. (See Table 3.) Of these, almost three out of five (58 percent, or 1,310 mentions) were individuals affiliated with the Church in one capacity or another, although not all supported official Church positions.

The hierarchy dominated Church voices in the news, with 571 citations. They accounted for over two out of every five Catholic sources (44 percent), and one out of four sources (26 percent) overall. As defined here, the hierarchy included all members of the clergy at or above the level of bishop. Lay Catholics made up the second most prominent group with 386 citations, accounting for over one out of four Catholic sources

(29 percent) and one out of six sources overall (17 percent). Priests and other members of religious orders counted for another 207 sources, representing one out of six Catholic sources (15 percent) and just under one out of ten (9 percent) overall. (Priests accounted for 69 percent of this source category and women religious 31 percent.) The only other major group of Catholic sources consisted of officials of Catholic schools, who appeared in 102 quotations.

Among non-Catholic sources, three groups were especially prominent. Government officials were quoted 172 times, accounting for just over one out of five (21 percent) non-Catholic sources overall. They were divided evenly between federal government officials, on one hand, and state and local officials on the other. The only other major non-Catholic groups to be quoted with any frequency were the leaders of other churches and religious scholars from outside the Catholic Church. The former were cited 108 times and the latter 104 times, each representing about one eighth of the non-Catholic total. There were no substantively significant differences across outlets in the patterns of sourcing that we encountered. For example, the proportion of sources from the Church hierarchy ranged only from a low of 21 percent at *USA Today* to a high of 34 percent at *U.S. News & World Report*.

In addition to categories of sources, we identified the individuals who were quoted most often. (See Table 4.) In light of the media's topical focus on the papacy, and the concentration of sourcing among the Church hierarchy, the results will come as no surprise. Pope John Paul II was the runaway winner with ninety quotations, more than four times that of the runnerup, New York's Cardinal O'Connor, who had twenty-one citations. Chicago's Cardinal Bernardin finished a close third with twenty quotes. The top ten list included seven cardinals, and the only individual outside the hierarchy to make the list was the prolific scholar and writer Father Andrew Greeley, who was quoted eleven times.

Presenting Church Teachings

Central to our inquiry is the debate over issues involving the Church and its teachings. In order to evaluate the media's presentation of substantive issues, we first needed to understand its overall parameters. So we sought to determine how often the Church's teachings were presented in the news, as well as the manner in which they were presented. In addition to the frequency of such reporting, we also measured how often these teachings were challenged or refuted by critics or opponents in the same story in which they were presented. To accomplish this, we examined every statement that was explicitly identified as representing the official Church view. Once this was noted, we examined the rest of the story to see if any other source argued against the Church teaching. This allowed us to differentiate between stories that simply recounted a Vatican statement and those that provided a broader context by including criticism of the doctrine.

We found that official Church teachings appeared very frequently in the news. (See Table 5.) A majority (56 percent) of all stories in the sample presented material that was specifically identified as official doctrine of the Church. For example, the following article from *Time* magazine not only stated Church doctrine on a range of social issues but the philosophy behind it:

> Evangelium Vitae, the Gospel of Life, is the 11th encyclical by Pope John Paul II, comprising his views on the most pressing moral issues facing the Roman Catholic Church and the world. He wrote to his brother bishops in 1991 asking for their ideas on the subject, and

their responses are reflected in his thoughtful writing. In the 17th year of his papacy, he sees new threats "on an alarmingly vast scale." While reaffirming the value and dignity of life, he is concerned with what he terms a prevailing "culture of death." He uncompromisingly persists in his condemnation of abortion, contraception and euthanasia, and decries the techniques of artificial reproduction.

The 189-page document, published last week, concludes that governments, as much as individuals, play a part in the tragedy unfolding around the globe. When the right to life is left to the will of the majority, John Paul preaches, democracy "effectively moves toward a form of totalitarianism." Society has a moral conscience, he argues, and must be guided by it. Appealing beyond his Catholic flock, he calls on political figures not to pass laws that disregard the dignity of the individual and thereby "undermine the very fabric of society."

—*Time*, April 10, 1995, p. 43

An additional 26 percent of all stories gave voice to Catholic clergy. These individuals sometimes presented the teachings of the Church without making a specific claim to speak for the Church. At other times they made noncontroversial comments on events or occurrences: For example, *U.S. News & World Report* ran an item on an on-line forum in which New York's Cardinal O'Connor used a laptop computer to discuss his views on matters ranging from television to theology. The article quotes his response to a Catholic homosexual with AIDS who was considering becoming an Episcopalian: "Clearly you should belong to the church you think God wants you to belong to" (*U.S. News & World Report*, January 16, 1995, p. 19). In another article, the eminently quotable Cardinal O'Connor echoed the sentiments of a participant at an open-air concert where young people from eight New York dioceses gathered for music, prayer, and religious exhibits. " 'I heard someone call this "Godstock," which I thought was impressive,' Cardinal O'Connor said" (*The New York Times,* August 15, 1994, p. B5).

If we combined the stories that explicitly identified the Church's teaching with those in which clergy implicitly echoed its teaching, about five stories out of six presented a representative of the Church's views on some issue, either with or without debate. Fewer than one story out of five (18 percent) failed to present the Church's view on some issues in any fashion.

Of course it might be argued that news about the Catholic Church almost by definition must present some statement of Church doctrine, whether as part of a debate or simply to explain the nature of a newsworthy event to non-Catholic audiences. Nonetheless, we found considerable variation across news genres in presenting official Church doctrine. The television networks proved least likely to present official Church positions. Only half (50 percent) of all TV news stories did so, with almost no variation across individual networks. At the other end of the spectrum were the weekly newsmagazines, which presented Church doctrines in nearly three out of four (72 percent) stories. Presumably this difference can be traced to the relative brevity forced upon television news stories compared to the length of presentation available to magazine writers.

However, this explanation cannot account for the differences we found among the newspapers in our sample. *USA Today,* which is well known for the brevity of its stories, proved even more likely than the newsmagazines to present official Church positions. Nearly three out of four (74 percent) *USA*

Today stories did so. *The Washington Post* was close behind with 70 percent of its stories. In sharp contrast *The New York Times,* famous for its in-depth treatment of the news, matched the networks, with only 50 percent of its stories presenting the Church's position. In fact, the *Times* was actually less likely than *CBS Evening News* (52 percent) to present Church teachings in its stories. Thus, it appears that the prominence of Church teachings in the news is related to presentation styles and editorial decisions as well as the exigencies of news formats.

The fact that news stories frequently presented statements of Church doctrine is important, but it does not tell us *how* doctrine was presented. The prominence of Church teachings helps to establish the extent of issue coverage, but it does not tell us whether doctrine was questioned or debated. It is also necessary to know how many of these stories included some debate over the teachings that were presented. Therefore, we examined every story to identify those in which one or more Church teachings were criticized or rejected. Among the 320 stories that presented an official Church doctrine, just over half (52 percent) did so without debate. (See Table 6.) In the remaining stories that debated Church policy, critics from outside the Church accounted for the largest source of alternative views — 28 percent, compared to 20 percent of stories that featured dissenters from within the Church.

Once again, this overall picture masks significant differences among the various media outlets. The outlets that were most likely to present Church teachings in the first place were also most likely to present dissent from those teachings. Conversely, the outlets that paid the least attention to Church doctrine were also least likely to present such doctrine in a controversial light. Perhaps reflecting its political orientation, *The Washington Post* was most likely to counter Church doctrines with dissenting viewpoints, doing so nearly two thirds (65 percent) of the time. Following close behind were the news-magazines, which differed little from one another, and collectively presented criticism 62 percent of the time that they printed Church teachings. *USA Today* also finished above the group average in presenting dissent, in 55 percent of relevant stories. All these outlets were notable for having covered Church positions in at least 70 percent of all articles about the Church.

The Washington Post highlighted dissent from official Catholic doctrine both within and outside the Church. For example, a story from U.S. Senator Edward Kennedy's 1994 re-election campaign invoked the ongoing battle over separating politics and religion:

> Sen. Edward M. Kennedy (D), a Catholic, and his Republican challenger, businessman Mitt Romney, a Mormon, have said they believe religion is a private matter, yet they have been repeatedly drawn into a collision of faith and politics.
>
> In the latest development, Kennedy has come under criticism from Cardinal Bernard Law of Boston, who rebuked the senator for saying he believes that women should be ordained as priests, a position at odds with Catholic doctrine.
>
> Earlier in the week, Kennedy, responding to a question from the Boston Globe, said he counts himself among "the growing number of Catholics who support the ordination of women as priests." Pope John Paul II recently reasserted the view that women may not be priests and that Catholics may not debate the subject.
>
> — *The Washington Post,* September 10, 1994, p. A3

A month later, the *Post* examined another conflict involving the position of women in the Church. Under the headline

"Nuns, Bishops Clash at Vatican Over the Role of Church-women," the *Post* reported on attempts of women religious to challenge authority at its highest source:

> The police who patrol St. Peter's Square could scarcely believe their eyes. Defying local laws, American nuns marched into the cavernous piazza last Saturday to carry their bold message straight to the windows of Pope John Paul II's apartment.
>
> Chanting "We shall not be silenced," the four nuns and several supporters raised banners that declared: "They are talking about us without us" and "Women want to be a part, not apart." Police quickly broke up the demonstration, confiscating the banners and detaining the nuns, who were released an hour later after identity checks.
>
> The protest dramatized one of the most controversial issues confronting the Roman Catholic Church — the pope's adamant refusal to alter the Vatican's male-dominated hierarchy and empower women with greater rights, including ordainment to the priesthood.
>
> — *The Washington Post,* October 27, 1994, p. A33

While noting the Church's official position on the ordination issue, the *Post* also stated the opposition's view: The Catholic Church has always insisted that it has no authority to ordain women as priests because Jesus Christ chose only men as his apostles. But women's rights groups contend that Christ was merely following the cultural norms of his time and that the Church should now accept the modern notion that women deserve to be accorded equal respect and treatment as men.

Extending the critique beyond ordination, "Doris Gottemoeller, head of the Sisters of Mercy of the Americas, told the bishops they should be more aware of 'feminist spirituality . . . as a sign of the times and a gift to the Church' " (*The Washington Post,* October 27, 1994, p. A33).

At the other end of the spectrum, we once again found an unlikely pairing of *The New York Times* and the network evening news shows. The three networks were sufficiently similar to be treated as a single entity. This odd couple gave relatively little notice to Church doctrine and even less to debate over that doctrine. When Church positions were presented, they were debated in network news stories only 37 percent of the time. The level of dissent or criticism was only slightly higher in *The New York Times*, appearing in 42 percent of relevant stories.

In general, then, we found that the news organizations that were most likely to cover doctrinal issues were also most likely to provide forums for dissent from them. What was less predictable was that the least issue oriented and conflictual reportage would appear in *The New York Times* and on the network evening news. It should be remembered, however, that these findings are based on the proportion of stories that fit into the relevant categories. Because the sheer number of stories about the Catholic Church was so high in *The New York Times,* a *Times* reader would have been exposed to a greater volume of debate than would readers or viewers of other national news outlets. It is only in terms of percentage differences that the *Times* slides down the scale.

Debating Church Doctrine and Practice

The battle of ideas involving the Church cannot be assessed fully from the distribution of topics and sources or the structure of stories involving Church teachings. It is necessary to examine directly how the news media presented the entire range of opinions on Church teachings and activities. In order to understand how the policies and teachings of the Catholic Church were viewed in the media, we analyzed all opinions by sources or reporters on thirty-six different issues related to Church life.

These issues included such frequently and heatedly debated topics as the status and role of women and minorities in the Church, the role of the laity, prohibitions of abortion, contraception and homosexual acts, debates over freedom of expression versus Church authority, Church-State relations, and ecumenism. In order for an opinion to be coded, the source or reporter had to make a clear appraisal of Church policy, stating agreement or disagreement with Church teachings. Ambiguous or unclear statements were not coded. Presenting the data separately on each of these thirty-six issues would be tedious and confusing, since many were addressed infrequently. Instead, we will present more general trends and examine views on particular issues only when they are noteworthy.

Most opinions clustered around five general areas of conflict. The most frequently discussed dimension dealt with power relations within the Church. This consisted of opinions on the following issues: the status and role of women (including their ordination), the status and role of minorities, the proper role for the laity, questions of academic freedom at Catholic institutions, changes in the Mass and other liturgical reforms, and appraisals of how the Church has handled dissenters.

A second dimension concerned Church stands on matters of sexual morality. This included opinions on five issue areas: prohibitions of abortion and artificial birth control, clerical celibacy, Church opposition to homosexual activity, and the moral and ethical problems posed by artificial reproductive technologies. A third dimension was constructed to deal with power relations between the Church and State authority. This included opinions in four distinct areas: questions of public funding for private schools, Church involvement in politics, Church teachings and policies regarding war, and the broader question of the proper separation of Church and State.

A fourth dimension dealt with ecumenism and relations among churches. This dimension included opinions on the desirability of Christian unity, obstacles to Christian unity, Catholic-Jewish relations, and relations between the Church and other faiths, especially the various Protestant denominations. The fifth and final dimension concerned various charges of wrongdoing directed at representatives of the Church. Most of these focused on alleged pedophilia by priests. A few stories dealt with how the Church handled sexual violations by the clergy. Other topics included drug abuse by priests and financial irregularities with Church funds.

The most extensive debate was over power relations within the Church. (See Table 7.) Issues related to authority, control, and dissent made up nearly half (45 percent) of all opinions that appeared on Church doctrine and practices. The great bulk of this debate revolved around the role of women in the Church. The second most frequent object of concentration concerned Church teachings on sexual morality. These made up just over one in five (22 percent) viewpoints that either criticized or defended Church teaching. Discussions of ecumenism were next in frequency, comprising 13 percent of the total. This point was followed closely by debates of allegedly illegal or immoral behavior by priests or members of the Church hierarchy. These emotionally charged debates accounted for one eighth (12 percent) of all opinions on Church policy and practices. The final category of Church-State relations accounted for about one out of twelve (8 percent) opinions that were voiced.

There was little variation across these news organizations in terms of the issues that were debated, but the exceptions to this pattern were sometimes notable. For example, the television network news shows were more likely to focus on sexual controversies (30 percent of all opinions) and charges of wrongdoing (16 percent) than most other outlets. But the networks' focus on allegations of illegality or immorality finished a distant second behind *USA Today,* which devoted 29 percent of its entire issue debate to this category — a level of coverage proportionately two and one half times as great as the overall average of all other outlets in the study.

Power Relations in the Church

Conflicts over power and authority in any major institution are treated as intrinsically newsworthy. So it is not surprising that the news media would give heavy coverage to issues of power and authority in the Catholic Church. What is surprising is the concentration of such coverage on a single controversy — the status of women in the Church. Out of 159 opinions that either supported current Church structures of authority or urged reforms, nearly eight out of ten (79 percent) concerned the position of women in the Church. By contrast, the proper role of the laity attracted only 4 percent of the commentary, as did the role of racial minorities in the Church. The Church's handling of all forms of internal dissent collectively accounted for only one opinion out of every eight (13 percent) that dealt with power relations. As we shall see, this narrow focus of debate over the "politics" of the Church was far more diverse in previous decades.

The concentration of debate on "women's issues" was nearly matched by the consensus of views expressed on these issues. Three out of four opinions on the role of women in the Church (75 percent) urged change or reform; only one out of four (25 percent) supported current practices. (See Table 8.) Voices urging reform were nearly unanimous on the television networks (94 percent in favor and only 6 percent opposed). Opinion was nearly as one-sided in the newsmagazines (82 percent favored reform) and *USA Today* (83 percent reformist). For example, in 1994, when the Synod of Bishops meeting in Rome issued a statement condoning greater authority for women in the Church, short of ordination, Bishop Pfeiffer appeared on ABC to say, "We humbly admit . . . that there is sexism in the Church, but we also clearly state that we are against it" (November 16, 1994). Another argument for change came from a 1997 *Newsweek* story on a resolution passed by the Catholic Theological Society of America challenging Cardinal Ratzinger's assertions of papal infallibility on the exclusion of women from the priesthood: "They argue that this practice was followed not out of obedience to 'the will of Jesus' but because of a common cultural conviction that 'women are inferior to men and more easily led astray.' . . . Morally, they claim the church's duty is to decide women's ordination based on what is authentically Christian and to discard mere cultural baggage" (June 16, 1997).

What little support there was for maintaining the status quo appeared mostly in the pages of the prestige press. *The New York Times* came closest to balanced coverage on the role of women, with 61 percent of opinions urging reform and 39 percent supporting the status quo, followed closely by *The Washington Post* at a 63 percent to 37 percent split. Thus, the *Times* quoted a member of the hierarchy who opposed the growing use of female servers at liturgy: " 'It is my honest opinion that less than 5 percent of the diocese is actively involved in having girls as servers.' When we hear about it, we send a letter asking him to refrain. . . . Should an individual priest be allowed to ban girl servers at his church? The diversity of opinions is not limited to the United States, Father Ginty said, which is why the pope left the decision up to his bishops. 'I doubt very much if churches in Eastern Europe, Asia or Africa are interested in female servers' " (June 12, 1994).

Apart from the representation of women, a smattering of

debate on the role of other groups and the treatment of dissenters produced a fairly even split of opinion. For example, *The Washington Post* quoted Paul Likoudis, news editor of the *Wanderer,* in opposition to Cardinal Bernardin's efforts to engage in a dialogue with reformers: "He seems to be abdicating the teaching and ruling authority he has for the sake of some ethical dialogue. It's time for sanctions against those who dissent, not dialogue" (August 17, 1996).

On the other side of this issue was a *Time* article on what the accompanying headline called "suppressing debate." The piece outlined numerous objections to the 1998 apostolic letter *Ad Tuendum Fidem* ("For the Defense of the Faith"), which restated the Church's positions on such issues as abortion, euthanasia, and the ordination of women. The article cited the case of a theologian who left the priesthood in protest against "the authorities in Rome . . . silencing all theological reflection and discussion." The reporter concluded, "The Vatican has abandoned the Inquisition, but still deals with what it sees as heresy by forbidding discussion and banning books" (November 2, 1998).

Sexuality and Morality

If gender issues topped the list of controversies covered by the national media in the 1990s, sexual issues were the clear runnerup. This category was also more diverse than the narrowly focused debate over power and authority relations. The debate over abortion accounted for about two out of five (41 percent) opinions in this sphere, the controversy over clerical celibacy for about one third (32 percent), and the debate over birth control about one fifth (19 percent). There was also a smattering of opinion on other issues related to sexuality, such as Church teachings on homosexuality and artificial reproductive technologies.

Debate on these topics was also significantly more balanced than we found with regard to gender issues. (See Table 9.) Among the sources who commented on Church doctrinal practice, a slight majority of 55 percent were critical, compared to 45 percent who supported the Church. However, this overall balance concealed the first significant difference we found between television and the print media. As noted above, television devoted much greater attention to issues of sexual morality than did newspapers and newsmagazines. We now find that television also provided the most negative portrayal of Church positions on these issues. On television news shows, 70 percent of all comments in this sphere were critical of the Church. By contrast, the print outlets collectively featured more support than criticism of the Church by 55 percent to 45 percent.

The print versus television split was most obvious with regard to the issues of abortion and clerical celibacy. The abortion issue has long been a lightning rod for the intersection of political controversy and Church doctrine. Perhaps because the two sides are so well defined, the coverage was quite balanced on this topic. In fact, a slight majority (56 percent) of sources supported the Church's position on abortion. On television news, however, nearly two out of three sources (62 percent) criticized Church teachings. Conversely, over two out of three print sources (68 percent) supported Church opposition to abortion.

It should be remembered that we were not examining all coverage of the abortion issue, only that component dealing with the Church's position on it. For example, *ABC World News Tonight* gave airtime to a doctor who, as the reporter put it, "says the Church has no business in setting medical policy" with regard to abortion. The doctor then appeared on screen to assert that abortion decisions should be a matter for a woman and her physician to determine: "Any third party entering the doctor-patient relationship . . . in my mind, they don't belong" (July 21, 1998). On the other side of this issue, ABC presented a representative of the Catholic Hospital Association to affirm the Church's role in this decision: "We will do our best to be faithful to who we are, never water down our commitment to life, never water down our commitment to human sexuality and the gift of reproduction" (July 21, 1998).

The issue of priestly celibacy was often raised in the context of debate over the difficulty in recruiting priests and the consequent shortage of clergy qualified to perform sacramental functions. For example, *ABC World News Tonight* quoted Tim Unsworth of the *National Catholic Reporter,* "If we had a married clergy we would have a surplus of priests in less than ten years" (January 18, 1998). *CBS Evening News* quoted a New Jersey parishioner in a similar vein, "There are many, many wonderful people who would make wonderful priests. I don't think we should deny them that. God works through a married person, through a woman, it doesn't matter" (October 4, 1995).

An article in *Time* magazine discussed this issue at length, presenting the same type of argument as those just noted but also citing a rebuttal from the prominent sociologist Father Andrew Greeley. "Yet some doubt the celibacy rule is responsible for the decline in the priesthood. It was never an easy cross to bear, they point out. Why should it be harder now than it has been throughout much of the church's 2,000-year history? 'People say the sexual revolution has made sex more attractive for young men,' Greeley observes. 'I say, give me a break!' " (October 9, 1995).

Among the major issues on sexual morality, only the debate over birth control produced consistent coverage across all news outlets. The overall coverage was balanced, with 47 percent supporting the Church's denunciation of artificial methods of birth control and 53 percent challenging this position. For example, *The Washington Post* described a Catholic couple who "see their children as the embodiment of their faith . . . they embrace John Paul II's bans on abortion and artificial contraception, which they say are based on the belief that all potential life is precious" (October 9, 1995).

On the other side of this issue, *Time* magazine writer Lance Morrow opined, "The Church is simply out to lunch on birth control. . . . Contraception sinlessly heads off the unwelcome pregnancy that might occasion the sin of abortion, that is, the destruction of rudimentary life. Only abstracted celibates and moral neurotics insist that a pill or condom contravenes the divine design for sex. On the contrary, contraception is an act of moral responsibility perfectly consistent with marital virtue" (October 3, 1994).

Ecumenism

Relations between the Roman Catholic Church and other religions comprised a third significant realm of debate in the media, while attracting less attention than the hot button issues related to power and sexuality. Apart from an occasional piece on Catholic-Jewish relations, the debate clustered around the topic of ecumenical outreach to other Christian faiths. The goal of Christian unity or broader ecumenical outreach was almost always seen as worthwhile. Debate flared as to whether the Church was doing enough to pursue this desirable goal.

For the most part, Church doctrines and practices were criticized as stumbling blocks on the road to Christian unity. (See Table 10.) A nearly unanimous 89 percent of all sources criticized Church doctrines and practices on this ground. In the newsmagazines not a single source defended the Church's ecumenical efforts. *The New York Times* and network news shows each presented only one source favoring the Church's position.

For example, *Newsweek* reported a 1997 speech by Eastern Orthodox Patriarch Bartholomew, which "warned an ecumenical audience that the separation between Catholics and Orthodox was not simply a matter of geography, organizational structure or juridical differences. . . . The patriarch seemed to be saying that the very way in which Catholics experience God — through prayer, the sacraments and doctrine — makes reunion impossible" (November 3, 1997). A far more benign view of the Catholic Church's ecumenical efforts appeared in a 1994 *Washington Post* story on the opening of diplomatic relations between the Vatican and Israel. The article described this as "the climax of . . . negotiations toward healing centuries of bitterness between Catholics and Jews." Reporter David Hoffman quoted an Israeli official's hope that the agreement "will help erase anti-Semitism and encourage the Church to play a more active role against it" (June 16, 1994).

Church-State Relations

If the Catholic Church was usually criticized for its relations to other religions, it fared considerably better in the debate over Church-State relations. Although discussions of the Church's relations with various levels of government in the United States received the least coverage of any dimension of the issue debate, the debate that did occur balanced criticisms with support for Church positions. (See Table 11.) This debate ranged from the perennial issue of whether tax revenues should be used to underwrite parochial schools to Church-sponsored public relations campaigns designed to affect public opinion and, at least indirectly, the legislative climate on issues important to the Church.

Overall, 48 percent of all sources supported the Church in its relation with government, and 52 percent expressed some criticism. This balance of opinion was uniform across all outlets, with no news organization tilting very far in either direction. For example, a *New York Times* article dealt with charges that Cardinal O'Connor was interfering in the 1996 presidential election campaign by criticizing President Clinton's veto of a bill banning partial-birth abortions. The *Times* quoted New York City Mayor Rudy Giuliani: "Such direct involvement in politics is not a good idea, because I think it confuses people. I think that religious institutions, including the Catholic Church, have every right to do everything they can to persuade their members and others as to their moral views. That can be done without focusing on a particular political figure, in this case the President of the United States" (*The New York Times,* April 22, 1996, p. B3).

However, the same article also quoted Cardinal O'Connor's vigorous defense, which included criticism of his critics: "It is a not-so-clever way of trying to muzzle the church. If the church here in New York, the church in Rome or anywhere else were to refrain to (sic) address such crucial issues of public policy simply because an election campaign is being waged, then the church would never be able to address these issues. The church will not be silenced simply because of an election."

Charges of Wrongdoing

Thus far we have considered what might be called the "issue debate" with regard to media coverage of the Catholic Church. This consists of evaluative statements in the news indicating either criticism or support for Church doctrine and practices. However, there was one major focal point of debate that revolved around questions of right and wrong rather than opinions pro and con. This last area of debate concerned the Church's response to charges of wrongdoing by its clergy. As we mentioned previously, much of this debate revolved around charges of pedophilia, including allegations against Cardinal Bernardin that were made and later retracted by a former altar boy.

We examined this debate insofar as it addressed the role of the Church as an institution. That is, we did not focus on questions of individual guilt or innocence but rather on the alleged complicity of the Church or the appropriateness of its response to such cases. Even in this relatively narrow context, charges of wrongdoing generated more debate than all issues in Church-State relations and nearly as much as the Church's relations to other religions. (See Table 12.) Moreover, media coverage of the Church's handling of such issues was largely negative. Among all sources who evaluated the Church in such contexts, 70 percent were critical of its responses and only 30 percent were supportive.

There was little variation across news outlets. Only *The Washington Post* provided evenly balanced coverage; all other outlets expressed reproach more often than approval of the Church's behavior. For example, in 1994 *The New York Times* conducted a poll that found that a majority of Catholics believed the Church was doing a poor job of handling charges of sexual abuse by priests. A *CBS Evening News* story on the poll quoted Father Richard McBrien of Notre Dame University, "I characterize their behavior as irresponsible and in some cases unconscionable insofar as they've turned on the victim" (May 5, 1994). Later that year *NBC Nightly News* aired a response to such charges from Bishop Thomas J. Costello: "I think we're working as honestly and openly on this admitted problem as we can" (November 14, 1994). But the nature of this topic lent itself to television's ability to communicate strong emotions and stories of personal injustice. For example, three years later, NBC aired a segment of an interview with a victim of sexual abuse in which he lamented, "I don't know what hurts more, the fact that it happened in the first place or the way the Catholic Church handled it" (July 25, 1997).

Characterizing the Church

The Church is more than the sum of its teachings, just as the news is more than the sum of the opinions that appear in a story. Thus, the media's depiction of the Catholic Church involves not only its presentation of policy issues in which the Church is involved, it also reflects the tone of news that is influenced by the use of descriptive language. For example, the tone of a story might be discursive, sarcastic, or ironic, depending upon the language chosen to convey the same factual information.

The entire journalistic endeavor is an attempt to describe events and ideas that the audience cannot experience directly. It is language (and, in the case of television, pictures) that guides the audience's vicarious experience of the reality that journalism describes. Therefore, our analysis extended to the use of descriptive terms that labeled or characterized the Church and its representatives. In contrast to determining the balance of opinions on particular issues, this represents a means of measuring more general depictions of Catholicism.

We were especially interested in words or phrases that carry emotive, judgmental, or value-laden connotations. To create the list of likely terms, we noted any use of emotive, colorful, or judgmental language while performing our initial qualitative analysis of the news. Based on a preliminary qualitative analysis that is described in our previous study, we isolated three terminological dimensions of language that characterized the Catholic Church: ideology (liberal versus conservative), control (oppressive versus liberating) and relevance (relevant versus irrelevant). These dimensions provided a means of measuring media descriptions of ideology in the Church, authority and control in the Church, and the Church's relevance to the modern world. By counting these words or phrases, we were able to assess the balance of descriptive language along the major dimensions on which the Church was characterized. (See Table 13.)

The ideological dimension noted conservative and liberal terms. On the conservative end were words like "reactionary," "retrogressive," and "traditional," while on the liberal side were "radical," "progressive," and "revolutionary." This dimension came into play most frequently when stories attempted to characterize candidates or new appointees to the hierarchy. The authority dimension separated words according to their characterization of the type of control exercised by the Church. On the "oppressive" end of this spectrum were such terms as "authoritarian" and "rigid"; on the opposite side were terms like "liberating," "unrestrictive," and "emancipating." The relevance dimension identified words that connoted something about the relevance of the Church in the world. Words connoting irrelevance were terms such as "outdated" and "anachronistic." On the opposite end of the spectrum were terms like "relevant" and "in touch."

Rather than count every emotive term that appeared, we measured the balance of such terms in each story. That is, we asked whether an entire story tended to characterize the Church mainly as liberal or conservative, liberating or oppressive, relevant or out of touch. Following previous scholarship, we adhered to a "two to one rule" in making this judgment. If twice as many words were drawn from one end of a dimension as from the other, the story was coded as tilted in that direction.

Ideology

We identified fifty-six stories, about one out of every ten in the sample, that labeled the Church or its leaders as liberal or conservative. Such descriptions were most likely to appear in *The New York Times* (twenty stories), followed by the newsmagazines (fourteen), and the television networks (thirteen). They were least likely to appear in *The Washington Post* (only seven stories) and *USA Today* (only twice). Regardless of the outlet, ideological characterizations of the Church usually emphasized its conservatism. Depictions of the Church's conservatism outnumbered those emphasizing its liberalism by nearly a four-to-one margin — 79 percent to 21 percent.

The tilt was most pronounced in the newsmagazines (93 percent conservative characterizations) and the network news shows (85 percent). For example, a 1994 *Time* magazine article speculating on who might be the next pope downplayed the chances of Cardinal Martini because "the conservative College of Cardinals is not likely to look kindly upon even a moderate member of an order [the Jesuits] with a reputation for liberalism" (December 26, 1994).

Authority

Stories that characterized the Church in terms of its authority structure usually emphasized its oppressive or authoritarian character. These kinds of depictions appeared nearly as frequently as did references to the conventional liberal-conservative ideological spectrum, appearing in forty-nine stories overall. The characterizations were almost as one-sided, with 78 percent referring to the oppressive nature of the Church and only 22 percent the liberating, or emancipatory, aspects of membership. Once again, the newsmagazines led in such character-izations with eleven depictions of the Church as authoritarian and none as liberating. The tilt was similar but less pronounced at other news outlets.

The precise terms were frequently more pointed or col-orful than the straightforward conservative-versus-liberal terms applied to the ideological spectrum. For example, a *Time* ar-ticle on Pope John Paul referred to him in the subhead as an "autocrat," and noted that liberal Catholics "see him as the prod-uct of a conservative, patriarchal church, which helps explain his increasingly autocratic and negative pronouncements. . . . These critics charge John Paul rules with an iron hand. . . ." An even more pointed depiction appeared in a *New York Times Sunday Magazine* article written by Father Andrew Greeley. Father Greeley wrote, "The Church is resolutely authoritarian, bishops and priests are authoritarian and insensitive" (June 10, 1994). (The point of Father Greeley's article was to show why Catholics remain in the Church despite such institutional fail-ings.)

Among the rare instances of the Church being character-ized as liberating rather than oppressing the individual was a profile of Maryknoll lay missionaries, who worked with the rural poor in Mexico. The article quoted one "missioner," as they call themselves: "Maryknoll missioners go overseas to work with poor people and help them build a profound experi-ence of church that is important to their lives and helps em-power them to reclaim their God-given dignity. That's a lot dif-ferent than beating people over the head with the Gospels and telling them to believe in Jesus Christ" (January 11, 1998).

Relevance

Compared to the domains of ideology of authority, char-acterizations of the Church's relevance proved rare. As we note below, such was not always the case. In previous decades, the Church's relevance to contemporary life was a more common focus of media characterization. Hence its inclusion in our study. In the 1990s, however, only eleven stories in the sample characterized the Church along this dimension, less than one quarter as frequently as characterizations of the Church's ideology and authority. Moreover, when such terms did appear, the results cut against the kind of terminology found most frequently in the other dimensions, which stressed its conservatism and even authoritarianism.

Trends in Coverage Over Time

How did the media's treatment of the Catholic Church in the 1990s compare to coverage from earlier decades? What continuities and changes did our research uncover in the Church's media image since Vatican II? To answer these questions, we made direct comparisons of our current findings with those of our previous study.

The two studies employed the same content analysis system and were conducted by the same researchers. The only difference was that we broadened the study's scope to include several additional media outlets in the 1990s. To ensure that all comparisons were appropriate, we restricted our long-term analysis to the four news organizations that were examined in both studies — *Time,* CBS, *The New York Times,* and *The Washington Post.* In the analysis that follows, when we refer to results from the 1990s, the conclusions are based on these four outlets alone.

Amount of Coverage

Coverage of Catholicism continued to decline during the 1990s, as it has in every decade since the 1960s. (See Table 14.) The 2,654 news items we identified from 1994 through

1998 represent a drop of 44 percent from the 4,691 items we counted from 1964 through 1968. In fact, this calculation understates the full decline in coverage. The 1960s total excludes CBS, because television news broadcasts were not yet archived.

However, most of this falloff occurred soon after the 1960s, when the sweeping reforms of Vatican II generated heavy press coverage. The coverage plummeted from an average of 938 items per year during the 1960s to only 554 per year during the 1970s. Since then the decline has been much more gradual, to 544 news items annually during the 1980s and 531 during the 1990s. Suffice it to say that the major media's much-noted resurgence of interest in religion and spirituality during the current decade has not extended to the Catholic Church.

Continuing declines in coverage at three of the four outlets were partially offset by an increase in coverage at *The New York Times* — the only increase at any outlet throughout the entire four decades of the study. The *Times* devoted 1,778 articles to the Church during the 1990s study period, up 30 percent from its 1,370 total during the comparable 1980s time period (but still down 37 percent from its peak of 2,840 articles during the 1960s). By contrast, *Time* published only 30 relevant stories during the most recent study period, down an astounding 80 percent from its 1960s total of 146 stories. *Washington Post* coverage was down 54 percent over the same period, and CBS was down 45 percent from its 1970s totals.

Topics

The 1990s saw some continuity but also significant shifts in topical focus as compared to the previous decades. (See Table 15.) Church happenings once again headed the top ten list of topics, accounting for more than a quarter of all news items reported. Similarly, news about the pope finished second on the list, just as it has ever since the 1970s, with forty-five mentions. This shows a distinct pattern of coverage over time that defines the Church primarily in terms of its leadership and its institutional activities. It also illustrates the media's tendency to cover the Church much like other major institutions, such as business, government, or interest groups, by reporting those official positions and events by which the institution defines itself.

But a significant new topic also appeared for the first time in the current study. Crimes committed by clerics — chiefly involving pedophilia — took the number three spot, accounting for one out of every twelve topics reported. Much of this coverage revolved around sexual abuse charges lodged against Cardinal Bernardin, which generated heavy publicity before they were retracted. But charges of sexual improprieties by priests, both homosexual and heterosexual in nature, became an ongoing story that transcended any particular case.

Another new topic on the top ten list concerned changes in the Church's population. These stories focused on the loss of members to other faiths, the continuing decline of priests and women religious, and the increase of Hispanic immigrants. The relation between religion and science also made the list for the first time. This topic focused on the general issue of tensions between science and faith, as well as the Church's position on evolving technologies of artificial reproduction.

Conversely, one notable change was the declining coverage of dissenters within the Church, which fell from fourth to eighth place in the 1990s. One possible explanation for this shift was the lack of an individual lightning rod such as Father Charles Curran. Alternatively, dissatisfied Church members may have left the Church or those dissenters who remained declined to speak out for fear of official discipline.

Other key topics from the past — civil rights, birth control, education, and relations with other religions — failed to make the top ten list in the current decade, although such issues continue to receive coverage as general news topics. What has changed is that the Church has become only one of several focal points of news about these issues. For example, while private education still commands media attention, the growth of non-Catholic Christian academies has shifted the focus of such stories away from Catholic parochial schools. Many other groups, both secular and religious, have stolen some of the Church's thunder on subjects such as birth control, abortion, and homosexuality. And while the Church helped lead the battle for racial integration in decades past, racial progress has diminished its role in that debate.

Sources

The balance of sources quoted by the media also changed in the 1990s (see Table 16), as the gap between Catholic and non-Catholic sources shrank from previous decades. While a majority of 58 percent were Catholic in our most recent sample, this was far less than the 70 percent we calculated in previous decades. This confirms our prior finding that the Church must compete for the media's attention with other groups that share some of its views on politically relevant topics, such as Protestant organizations that make up the so-called Christian Right. As long as reporters can quote some representative of a particular position (for example, anti-abortion), they may not feel obliged to include a statement from the Church. In addition, researchers, professors, and scholars who are not identified as Catholic increased their representation among outside sources.

Among Catholic sources, the Church hierarchy continued to dominate in the coverage, although its visibility declined slightly (to 44 percent in the 1990s, versus 55 percent previously). Priests and women religious fell from second to third place, while the laity gained in prominence. Lay Catholics jumped from third to second place in the 1990s, and their share among all Catholic sources more than doubled, from 13 percent in past decades to 31 percent in the current decade. Among the declining proportion of priests and religious quoted in news accounts, the majority (62 percent) were males, solidifying a predominantly male presence among Catholic sources. The changing face of Catholicism in the media probably reflects two trends: the shrinking ranks of priests and religious, many of whom have left their positions, died, or retired; and the increased presence of lay Catholics assuming some of the functions once performed by clergy.

Among non-Catholic sources, representatives of state and local governments held a slight edge over the leaders from other churches, who headed the list in decades past. Federal officials took third place on the most recent list, dropping a notch from our earlier study. This trend reflects the local focus of the school prayer and voucher debates, as well as the prosecution of priests charged with criminal behavior in state and local jurisdictions. Other related discussions include the issue of whether specific local or state politicians — like mayors or governors — can express opinions that contradict the Church and still be considered Catholic.

In addition to general groups of sources, we also analyzed the prominence of particular individuals in the news. (See Table 17.) As in previous decades, coverage was dominated by the Church hierarchy, especially the pope. In the 1990s, John Paul II received ninety citations (fifty-six when citing only the usual four comparison outlets; see also Table 4), more than four times the amount of any other source. This reflects not only his position as head of the Church but also his many foreign trips, which are natural news events, as well as his facility with the media. With the exception of novelist-sociologist Andrew Greeley, bishops, archbishops, and cardinals comprised the major voices of the Church. Among them, Cardinal O'Connor and the late Cardinal Bernardin topped the list, each receiving more than twice the coverage of any other prince of the Church. In contrast to previous decades, Father Charles Curran was notably absent from the recent list. This change reflects the decline in coverage relating to doctrinal dissent, which Father Curran symbolized.

Presenting Church Teachings

Another recent shift in coverage involved the question of whether stories presented the Church's official position. (See Table 18.) In fact the current decade contained the highest proportion of stories noting the Church's position, fully 56 percent compared to the low of 37 percent in the 1980s, 40 percent in the 1970s, and 43 percent in the 1960s. This reflects trends we already noted — the dominance of the official Church among Catholic sources, the diminished voice of dissenters, and the media's tendency to cover the Church as an institution by reporting its official position.

However, the fact that the Church's position was noted did not mean that it went unchallenged. Out of 224 stories that stated the Church's position in the 1990s, fewer than half (46 percent) simply stated doctrine or announcements without additional comment, about the same proportion as in the past. (See Table 19.) In the remaining 54 percent of stories, the Church's position was challenged with roughly equal frequency from internal critics and those outside the Church. This represents a shift from our initial study, when dissent was more than three times as likely to come from internal than external sources (39 percent versus 11 percent).

The level of consensus was even greater in stories where the clergy expressed their views. In this category, nearly four in five stories (79 percent) generated no debate, a substantial increase over the two in five items from the past. In earlier times, critics of the clergy's positions were about twice as likely to originate inside the Church (23 percent versus 12 percent). More recently, criticism was equally divided between internal and external sources, with each accounting for just under 10 percent of all views expressed by the clergy. Thus, the decline of publicized dissent from within the Church was counterbalanced by an increase in criticism from without.

Debating Church Doctrine and Practice

We also examined the relative frequency of debate on Church positions by each time period for this study. (See Table 20.) The analysis confirmed the temporary rise in the coverage of dissent during the 1980s, as we noted in our previous discussion of topics. Fully 58 percent of stories during that decade featured debate on Church positions. In contrast, fewer than half the stories on this subject from the 1960s, 1970s, and 1990s noted controversy over official Catholic teachings and pronouncements.

The 1990s brought a major change in the focus of debate. (See Table 21.) Media attention shifted away from issues of Church teachings involving sexual morality (such as abortion, birth control, and priestly celibacy), which had generated continuous debate ever since Vatican II. The proportion of opinions expressed on such issues dropped by almost half, from 30 percent during the 1960s through the 1980s to 16 percent in the 1990s.

Conversely, the proportion of opinions expressed on the structure of power and authority within the Church nearly doubled, from 22 percent to 42 percent in the same time periods. This increase was entirely due to the increasingly heated debate over the role of women in the Church. Even as earlier debates over the role of racial minorities and the laity faded from view, these issues were replaced by criticism of the patriarchal nature of the hierarchy and arguments over the ordination of women. This single-issue focus catapulted the general topic of the distribution of power from the third most heavily debated area in past decades to the number one source of controversy in the 1990s.

Two other areas of controversy also gained a higher profile during the 1990s. First, debate over ecumenism rose from 13 to 23 percent of all opinions expressed. This reflects renewed attention to Catholic-Jewish relations on topics ranging from the Church's activities with regard to the Holocaust to the canonization of Edith Stein. Second, viewpoints on Church-State relations more than doubled from 5 to 12 percent of all opinions expressed. Increased debate in this area reflects the phenomenon of Catholic politicians (such as Senator Edward Kennedy) making news by opposing Church positions, as well as the Church's direct engagement with political issues such as abortion and euthanasia.

Finally, an area of controversy that emerged afresh in the 1990s was that of wrongdoing by representatives of the Church. As noted above, debate over the Church's role in dealing with wrongdoing (as opposed to purely individual culpability) had arisen too infrequently to be accorded separate treatment in our earlier study. During the current decade, by contrast, this highly charged area accounted for one out of every fourteen opinions (7 percent) expressed in all controversial areas. Even so, it was relatively less prominent as a source of debate than as a purely topical focus of news.

Viewpoints on sexual morality were almost perfectly balanced between support for and opposition to Church teachings during the 1990s. This pattern has remained constant ever since the 1970s. (See Table 22.) Only in the 1960s did Church teachings stimulate widespread opposition in the media, with two out of three sources voicing opposition. Much of the criticism of that time was in response to Church teachings forbidding the use of artificial methods of contraception. During the 1990s, viewpoints on birth control were relatively balanced (45 percent positive and 55 percent negative toward Church teachings). The Church's position on abortion actually received fairly strong support, with 61 percent positive and only 39 percent negative comments. The heaviest criticism was reserved for the policy of priestly celibacy, which was supported by only 36 percent of sources and opposed by 64 percent. Yet even this distribution of opinion was slightly more favorable to the Church than our results from previous decades, which produced a combined 27 percent support and 73 percent opposition.

Despite the newfound prominence of this debate, views on the Church power structure also remained steady over time. (See Table 23.) Two out of three sources (66 percent) favored reform during the 1960s and 1970s, a proportion that dropped to 60 percent in the 1980s, but rose again to 71 percent in the 1990s. Despite this consistency in the tone of this debate, the amount of debate increased after the 1960s, as many stories presented sources wrestling with the implications of Vatican II reforms. As noted above, by the 1990s the number of viewpoints evaluating the Church power structure was more than double that of the 1960s. Thus, reformers became more prominent in the news, if not more dominant.

The 1990s saw a decided shift in coverage of how the Church treats various groups. As noted above, this debate concentrated almost entirely on the role of women. Seventy percent of viewpoints favored changing the status of women, up from 56 percent in previous decades. Many of the criticisms came from sources favoring women's ordination, as well as those expressing more general dissatisfaction with the Church's treatment of women. Topics such as Church treatment of mi-

215

norities and the laity were debated too infrequently in the 1990s to draw comparisons with previous decades.

While viewpoints on the need for change in the Church remained fairly constant over the four decades covered by this study, there were some significant shifts among individual media outlets. About two thirds of views in *The Washington Post* and *The New York Times* advocated change, echoing the trend of previous decades. But in *Time,* approval of reform jumped from 63 percent in previous decades to 82 percent in the current decade. All views recently expressed on CBS favored change, compared to two out of five in previous decades. However, the number of opinions expressed was very low, rendering comparisons over time statistically meaningless.

There was also a notable shift on the Church's role in promoting religious unity. (See Table 24.) Among those expressing explicit opinions on this issue, three quarters viewed the Church as an obstacle to the union of different faiths, compared to half of all opinions expressed in the past. Current conflict focused mainly on Catholic-Jewish relations, specifically the Church's limited admission of guilt during the Holocaust, as well as the controversy caused by the canonization of Jewish-born nun Edith Stein.

The two remaining areas of debate were not relevant in this comparison. The distribution of viewpoints on the Church's involvement in politics differed little from the pattern we observed during the previous decade, but so few opinions were expressed in the four outlets as to render comparisons meaningless. In the case of the Church's response to wrongdoing by its representatives, data were not collected prior to the 1990s.

Characterizing the Church

Finally, in the case of terminological characterizations of the Church, differences appeared over time in both frequency and tone. In the case of ideological labeling, while the split remained consistent over time — with about two thirds of stories calling the Church conservative versus one third that called it liberal — the overall use of such labels fell significantly. (See Table 25.) Despite our use of more rigorous data collection techniques now available through computerized word pattern searches, only thirty-six stories in the 1990s were found to portray the Church as conservative or liberal, compared to ninety-five in the 1980s. The media were over three times more likely to present such labels in the 1960s (127 stories), when ideological tags were most frequently employed.

There was a similar decline in the tendency to label the Church as either an oppressive or liberating institution. (See Table 26.) The use of such terms dropped from forty stories in the 1980s to twenty-four stories in the 1990s. The same pattern occurred from the 1960s to the 1970s, when such stories fell from forty-six to twenty-nine, before rebounding in the 1980s. Critics were more likely to call the Church oppressive in the last two decades of this study. All relevant stories in the 1980s and 1990s contained language critical of the Church's control of its members, versus about three quarters of such stories in the 1960s and 1970s. Roughly a quarter of stories presented the Church as liberating during those decades, an image that has virtually disappeared since 1980.

Ever since Vatican II, theologians, lay Catholics, and non-Catholics have vigorously debated the modern relevance of this two-thousand-year-old institution. Still, the prominence of this terminology in news stories fell from a high of thirty-two stories in the 1960s to only six stories in the current decade. (See Table 27.) But even as coverage declined, as we noted earlier, its tone became more positive. In the 1990s, over 90 percent called the Church relevant to contemporary concerns. In earlier decades, verbiage portraying the Church as a relevant institution represented a distinct minority of all characterizations. Ironically, characterizations of the Church's relevance themselves became less relevant to the coverage, even as they became more positive in tone.

By contrast, ten stories described the Church as relevant and only one as irrelevant to contemporary life. For example, on the fiftieth anniversary of Pope John Paul II's ordination as a priest, *USA Today* interviewed a theologian at Georgetown University, asking him how the Roman Catholic Church had changed since the pope was ordained. He replied, "The Church is very different today. . . . The Second Vatican Council helped to update the Church to face the issues of the modern world. . . . The Church is much more concerned with social justice. It's more ecumenical" (November 1, 1996).

Conclusion

The twin goals of this study were to understand how the national media have portrayed the Catholic Church in the 1990s and to interpret the results within the context of long-term trends in the Church's media image. To accomplish this, we examined several dimensions of news coverage by nine nationally influential print and broadcast news organizations. These dimensions included the news topics, the sources who were cited, the presentation of Church teachings, the debates over controversies in which the Church was involved, and the descriptive language that was employed to characterize the Church.

These elements of news stories were subjected to a scientific content analysis of the broadcast network evening newscasts, the leading weekly newsmagazines, and the most nationally influential general interest newspapers from 1994 through 1998. The results were compared to those from our earlier study of media coverage from the 1960s through the 1980s, with direct comparisons of coverage in the four news outlets included in both the current and previous studies — *The New York Times, The Washington Post, Time* magazine, and *CBS Evening News.*

The results demonstrate the persistence of several long-term trends in the coverage, while highlighting some distinguishing characteristics of the national media's current portrayal of the Catholic Church. Among the long-term trends across the past four decades were: (1) declining coverage; (2) a focus on a few broad areas of controversy (these included power relations within the Church, teachings on sexual morality, and the Church's relation to the political system and to other religions); and (3) a preference for critics who contend that the Church needs to be more inclusive toward its own constituencies, such as women and minorities, and toward other religions.

The 1990s were distinguished by a concentrated focus on debate over the role of women in the Church, with a corresponding shift away from such long-running debates as abortion, birth control, and the treatment of doctrinal dissenters. The voices of internal dissenters were increasingly replaced in the news by those of external critics. Equally significant was the unprecedented level of attention given to charges of criminal behavior by clerics, with particular emphasis on charges of pedophilia and sexual abuse. The topical focus on this explosive subject was accompanied by heavy criticism of the Church's institutional response to charges of individual wrongdoing.

The opinion debate over Church teachings and activities also changed during the 1990s. In previous decades, debate had centered on Church doctrines with regard to sexual morality. Authority issues played a secondary role and encompassed several controversies, including the appropriate roles of the laity, women, homosexuals, and racial minorities. During the current decade, debate coalesced around the role of women. This included both questions of ordination and the general status of women in the Church.

The new prominence of women's rights issues was especially important to overall perceptions of the Church, because this proved to be an area in which the media debate was sharply tilted in favor of change. In contrast to such contentious issues as sexual morality and Church-State relations, on which opinion was roughly balanced, three out of four sources supported reforms that would give more authority to women. Opinions were equally critical of the Church's relations with other religions. Overall, current Church teachings or practices received less support in the 1990s than they had in the previous decade.

Finally, although the Church continued to be described primarily in terms connoting ideological conservatism and oppressiveness, the use of such terms declined markedly from previous decades. But this decline also meant that the Church was rarely characterized in terms of its relevance to contemporary life. When such depictions did appear, they were more likely to portray the Church as relevant, in contrast to previous decades.

On the whole, national media coverage of the Catholic Church in the 1990s continued to treat it primarily within a framework of political news. This applied to both its external relations to political issues and institutions and its internal authority structures. As it has over the past four decades, the coverage again emphasized the need for the Church to adapt to the more egalitarian and democratic norms and procedures that characterize the secular institutions of American society. In the 1990s, this perspective focused mainly on the Church's treatment of women and heightened attention to clerical wrongdoing. As we found in our earlier study, this was not matter of overtly opinionated or muckraking coverage. It would be more accurate to see it as the reflection of the prism through which one institution — the media — views another with very different norms and traditions.

The Center for Media and Public Affairs is a nonprofit, nonpartisan research and educational organization that conducts scientific studies of the news and entertainment media. CMPA election studies have played a major role in the ongoing debate over improving the election process. Since its formation in 1985, CMPA has emerged as a unique institution that bridges the gap between academic research and the broader domains of media and public policy.

TABLE 1
TOTAL NUMBER OF NEWS ITEMS

Television		**216**
ABC	77	
CBS	69	
NBC	70	
Magazines		**67**
Time	30	
Newsweek	21	
U.S. News & World Report	16	
Newspapers*		**2820**
The New York Times	1778	
The Washington Post	777	
USA Today	265	
Total		**3103**

* The study analyzed a 10 percent random sample of newspaper articles.

TABLE 2
LEADING TOPICS

Topic	Number of Stories	Percentage
Church Happenings	239	34
News of the Pope	99	14
Crimes by Clerics	58	8
Church in Politics	45	6
Changing Church Population	35	5
Canon Law	35	5
Abortion	33	5
Church and Science	27	4
Relations With Other Religions	24	3
Women's Issues	21	3
Dissent in Church	20	3
Education	16	2

TABLE 3
SOURCES CITED

Source	Number	Percentage
Church Hierarchy	571	26
Lay Catholics	386	17
Priests and Religious	207	9
Catholic Schools	102	5
Other	44	1
Total Catholic Sources	**1310**	**58%**
Leaders of Other Churches	108	5
Religious Scholars	104	5
Federal Government	86	4
State/Local Governments	86	4
Other	548	24
Total Non-Catholic Sources	**932**	**42%**
Total Sources	**2242**	**100%**

TABLE 4
LEADING INDIVIDUAL SOURCES CITED

	Number of Citations
Pope John Paul II	90
Cardinal O'Connor	21
Cardinal Bernardin	20
Father Andrew Greeley	11
Cardinal Law	9
Cardinal Mahony	9
Cardinal Keeler	8
Cardinal Ratzinger	7
Cardinal Hickey	4
Pope Pius XII	4
Bishop Pilla	4

TABLE 5
PRESENTATION OF CHURCH POSITION BY OUTLET

	Official Doctrine	Clergy Position	No Position	Total	Number of Stories
ABC	49	30	21	100%	77
CBS	52	28	20	100%	69
NBC	47	33	20	100%	70
Time	77	13	10	100%	30
Newsweek	62	14	24	100%	21
U.S. News & World Report	75	12.5	12.5	100%	16
USA Today	74	11	15	100%	27
The Washington Post	70	18	13	100%*	79
The New York Times	50	31	19	100%	180
Total	56	26	18	100%	569

*Does not add up to 100% due to rounding.

TABLE 6
DEBATE OF CHURCH POSITIONS

	No Debate	Internal Debate	External Critics	Total	Number of Stories
ABC	55	13	32	100%	38
CBS	61	19	19	100%*	36
NBC	73	9	18	100%	33
Time	35	26	39	100%	23
Newsweek	38	31	31	100%	13
U.S. News & World Report	42	50	8	100%	12
USA Today	45	10	45	100%	20
The Washington Post	35	29	36	100%	55
The New York Times	58	17	26	100%*	90
Total	52	20	28	100%	320

*Does not add up to 100% due to rounding.

TABLE 7
AREAS OF DEBATE
(PERCENT OF OPINIONS)

	TV News	Magazines	USA Today	The Washington Post	The New York Times	All Outlets
Power Structures	37	49	29	51	48	45
Sexual Morality	30	15	24	26	14	22
Ecumenism	8	20	4	8	18	13
Wrongdoing	16	8	29	10	9	12
Church-State	9	8	14	5	11	8
	100%	100%	100%	100%	100%	100%
Number of Opinions	100	78	21	77	81	357

TABLE 8
VIEWPOINTS ON ROLE OF WOMEN IN THE CHURCH

	TV News	Magazines	USA Today	The Washington Post	The New York Times	All Outlets
Criticize Church	94	82	83	63	61	75
Support Church	6	18	17	37	39	25
	100%	100%	100%	100%	100%	100%
Number of Opinions	33	34	6	30	23	126

TABLE 9
VIEWPOINTS ON CHURCH TEACHINGS
ON SEXUAL MORALITY

	TV News	Magazines	USA Today	The Washington Post	The New York Times	All Outlets
Criticize	70	50	40	55	20	55
Support	30	50	60	45	80	45
	100%	100%	100%	100%	100%	100%
Number of Opinions	30	12	5	20	10	77

TABLE 10
VIEWPOINTS ON CHURCH'S ECUMENICAL ROLE

	TV News	Magazines	USA Today	The Washington Post	The New York Times	All Outlets
Church Is Obstacle	86	100	0	60	91	89
Church No Obstacle	14	0	0	40	9	11
	100%	100%	100%	100%	100%	100%
Number of Opinions	7	13	0	5	11	36

TABLE 11
VIEWPOINTS ON CHURCH'S INVOLVEMENT IN POLITICS

	TV News	Magazines	USA Today	The Washington Post	The New York Times	All Outlets
Appropriate	44	67	0	50	56	48
Inappropriate	56	33	100	50	44	52
	100%	100%	100%	100%	100%	100%
Number of Opinions	9	6	3	4	9	31

TABLE 12
VIEWPOINTS ON CHURCH'S HANDLING
OF CHARGES OF WRONGDOING

	TV News	Magazines	USA Today	The Washington Post	The New York Times	All Outlets
Support	31	17	33	50	14	30
Criticize	69	83	67	50	86	70
	100%	100%	100%	100%	100%	100%
Number of Opinions	16	6	6	8	7	43

TABLE 13

CHARACTERIZATIONS OF THE CHURCH

Ideology		Authority		Relevance	
Liberal	21	Empowering	22	Relevant	91
Conservative	79	Oppressive	78	Irrelevant	9
	100%		100%		100%
Number of Stories	56	Number of Stories	49	Number of Stories	11

TABLE 14
TOTAL NUMBER OF STORIES
FOR EACH OUTLET BY DECADE
(FOUR COMPARISON OUTLETS ONLY)

	1960s	1970s	1980s	1990s	Total
CBS	—	126	105	69	300
Time	146	70	43	30	289
The Washington Post*	1705	1265	1200	777	4947
The New York Times*	2840	1310	1370	1778	7298
Total	4691	2771	2718	2654	12,834
Annual Average	938	554	544	531	

* A random sample of 10 percent of newspaper articles was selected for the content analysis.

TABLE 15
TOP TEN TOPICS BY DECADE
(FOUR COMPARISON OUTLETS ONLY)

	Number of Stories	Percentage of Stories
1960s		
Church Happenings	238	31
Birth Control	106	14
Changes in Canon Law	95	12
Relations With Other Religions	82	11
Dissent Within the Church	81	11
Education	68	9
Civil Rights	53	7
News of the Pope	46	6
Vietnam War	41	5
Economic Issues	30	4
1970s		
Church Happenings	161	28
News of the Pope	112	19
Abortion	57	10
Relations With Other Religions	46	8
Education	43	7
Church in Politics	40	7
Women in Church	39	7
Changes in Canon Law	33	6
Crimes by Clerics	21	4
Dissent Within the Church	20	3
1980s		
Church Happenings	152	29
News of the Pope	71	14
Dissent Within the Church	63	12
Relations With Other Religions	48	9
Abortion	41	8
Education	39	7
Economic Issues	37	7
Church and Politics	36	7
Women in the Church	27	5

Table 15 (continued)		
Homosexuality	21	4
1990s		
Church Happenings	131	26
News of the Pope	42	8
Crimes by Clerics	39	8
Sex Crimes	(32)	(6)
Church and Politics	24	5
Canon Law	22	4
Changing Church Populations	21	4
Abortion	21	4
Dissent Within the Church	18	4
Church and Science	16	3
Women in the Church	16	3

TABLE 16
SOURCES CITED IN STORIES ABOUT THE
CATHOLIC CHURCH IN THE 1990S
(FOUR COMPARISON OUTLETS ONLY)

	Number of Citations
Church Hierarchy	398
Lay Catholics	279
Priests and Religious	139
Catholic Schools	22
Catholic Media	19
Catholic Dissidents	3
Total Catholic Sources	**860**
Leaders of Other Churches	70
Federal Government	62
State/Local Government	74
Foreign Government	14
Abortion Rights Groups	11
Anti-Abortion Groups	14
All Others	3959
Total Non-Catholic Sources	**4204**

TABLE 17
LEADING INDIVIDUAL SOURCES CITED IN THE 1990s
(FOUR COMPARISON OUTLETS ONLY)

	Number of Citations
Pope John Paul II	56
Cardinal John O'Connor	14
Cardinal Joseph Bernardin	10
Father Andrew Greeley	8
Cardinal Roger Mahony	7
Archbishop Bernard Law	6
Cardinal Joseph Ratzinger	6
Cardinal William Keeler	6
Bishop Anthony Pilla	3
Archbishop Rembert Weakland	3
Cardinal James Hickey	3

TABLE 18
PRESENTATION OF CHURCH POSITION BY DECADE

	1960s	1970s	1980s	1990s
Church Position Presented	43	40	37	56
Catholic Clergy Position Presented	31	32	44	26
No Position	26	28	19	18
	100%	100%	100%	100%
Number of Stories	763	648	465	358

TABLE 19
PRESENTATION OF DEBATE IN STORIES
IDENTIFYING CHURCH POSITION IN THE 1990S
(FOUR COMPARISON OUTLETS ONLY)

	Church Position	Clergy View	No View
No Debate	46	79	83
Internal Debate	25	10	8
Other Critics	29	11	9
	100%	100%	100%
Number of Stories	224	96	63

TABLE 20
DEBATE OF CHURCH POSITIONS BY DECADE
(FOUR COMPARISON OUTLETS ONLY)

	Debate Percent of Stories	No Debate Percent of Stories		Number of Stories
1960s	49	51	100%	335
1970s	43	57	100%	233
1980s	58	42	100%	195
1990s	45	55	100%	354

TABLE 21
AREAS OF DEBATE
PERCENT OF VIEWPOINT ON CHURCH POSITIONS
(FOUR COMPARISON OUTLETS ONLY)

	1990s	1960s-1980s
Power Structures	42	22
Ecumenism	23	13
Sexual Morality	16	30
Church-State	12	5
Charges of Wrongdoing	7	—

TABLE 22
VIEWPOINTS ON SEXUAL MORALITY BY DECADE
(FOUR COMPARISON OUTLETS ONLY)

	Support Percent of Views	Criticize Percent of Views		Number of Opinions
1960s	36	64	100%	132
1970s	56	44	100%	52
1980s	52	48	100%	65
1990s	51	49	100%	47

TABLE 23
VIEWPOINTS ON THE
CHURCH POWER STRUCTURE BY DECADE
(FOUR COMPARISON OUTLETS ONLY)

	Favor Change	Favor Status Quo		Number of Opinions
1960s	66	34	100%	38
1970s	66	34	100%	71
1980s	60	40	100%	75
1990s	71	29	100%	78

TABLE 24
VIEWPOINTS ON THE CHURCH'S ECUMENICAL ROLE
(FOUR COMPARISON OUTLETS ONLY)

	Positive	Negative		Number of Opinions
1960s-1980s	50	50	100%	24
1990s	25	75	100%	24

TABLE 25
IDEOLOGICAL CHARACTERIZATIONS OF THE CHURCH BY DECADE (FOUR COMPARISON OUTLETS ONLY)

	"Conservative"	"Liberal"		Number of Stories
1960s	59	41	100%	127
1970s	66	34	100%	77
1980s	65	35	100%	95
1990s	67	33	100%	36

TABLE 26
CHARACTERIZATIONS OF CHURCH CONTROL BY DECADE
(FOUR COMPARISON OUTLETS ONLY)

	"Oppressive"	"Liberating"		Number of Stories
1960s	76	24	100%	46
1970s	79	21	100%	29
1980s	100	0	100%	40
1990s	96	4	100%	24

TABLE 27
CHARACTERIZATIONS OF THE RELEVANCE
OF THE CHURCH BY DECADE
(FOUR COMPARISON OUTLETS ONLY)

	"Irrelevant"	"Relevant"		Number of Stories
1960s	66	34	100%	32
1970s	60	40	100%	10
1980s	80	20	100%	15
1990s	0	100	100%	6

Edited by Patrick Riley
and Russell Shaw

ANTI-
CATHOLICISM

IN THE

MEDIA

An examination of whether
elite news organizations
are biased against the Church

An in-depth examination of media bias and
the Catholic Church in the United States.
0-87973-**551**-1, hardcover, $16.95, 256 pp.

To order from Our Sunday Visitor:
Toll free: 1-800-348-2440
E-mail: osvbooks@osv.com
Website: www.osv.com

Prices and availability of books subject to change without notice.

Anti-Catholicism in the American experience with a
special focus on abortion and private schools.
0-87973-**529**-5, hardcover, $14.95, 320 pp.

To order from Our Sunday Visitor:
Toll free: 1-800-348-2440
E-mail: osvbooks@osv.com
Website: www.osv.com

Prices and availability of books subject to change without notice.

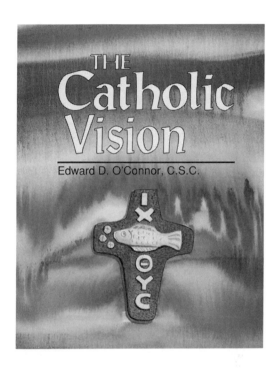

By presenting the mystery of God and the Church, a
basic understanding is gained of how the Faith can be
integrated into one's personal life.
0-87973-**736**-0, paper, $15.95, 480 pp.
0-87973-**418**-3, hardcover, $19.95, 480 pp.

To order from Our Sunday Visitor:
Toll free: 1-800-348-2440
E-mail: osvbooks@osv.com
Website: www.osv.com

Catholicism and Secularization in America

EDITED BY
David L. Schindler

Essays on Nature, Grace, and Culture

Louis Bouyer
Louis Dupré
Walter Kasper
Michael Novak
Glenn W. Olsen
David L. Schindler
Kenneth L. Schmitz

The relationship between Catholic Faith
and human culture is explored.
0-87973-**450**-7, paper, $7.95, 220 pp.

To order from Our Sunday Visitor:
Toll free: 1-800-348-2440
E-mail: osvbooks@osv.com
Website: www.osv.com

Our Sunday Visitor. . .

Your Source for Discovering the Riches of the Catholic Faith

Our Sunday Visitor has an extensive line of materials for young children, teens, and adults. Our books, Bibles, booklets, CD-ROMs, audios, and videos are available in bookstores worldwide. To receive a FREE full-line catalog or for more information, call **Our Sunday Visitor** at **1-800-348-2440**. Or write, **Our Sunday Visitor** / 200 Noll Plaza / Huntington, IN 46750.

- -

Please send me: ___A catalog
Please send me materials on:
___Apologetics and catechetics   ___Reference works
___Prayer books   ___Heritage and the saints
___The family   ___The parish

Name_____

Address_____Apt._____

City_____State____Zip_____

Telephone (   ) _____

A93BBABP

- -

Please send a friend: ___A catalog
Please send me materials on:
___Apologetics and catechetics   ___Reference works
___Prayer books   ___Heritage and the saints
___The family   ___The parish

Name_____

Address_____Apt._____

City_____State____Zip_____

Telephone (   ) _____

A93BBABP

- -

Our Sunday Visitor
200 Noll Plaza
Huntington, IN 46750
Toll free: 1-800-348-2440
E-mail: osvbooks@osv.com
Website: www.osv.com
   Your Source for Discovering the Riches of the Catholic Faith